Careers *with* Animals

The Humane Society of the United States

written by
Willow Ann Sirch

fulcrum resources
Golden, Colorado

The Humane Society of the United States
2100 L Street, NW, Washington, DC 20037
©1996 The HSUS. All rights reserved.

Dedicated to William D. Soltow, Jr.

Copyright © 2000 The Humane Society of the United States

Cover illustration © 2000 Ann W. Douden

Interior photographs (and illustration) appear courtesy of: page 12, copyright © 2000 Pamela Burns; page 17, copyright © 2000 Belinda Lewis; page 21, copyright © 2000 Kathryn Destreza; page 25, copyright © 2000 David Garcia; page 30, copyright © 2000 Barbara Scanlon; page 35, copyright © 2000 Earlene Cole; page 39, copyright © 2000 Dr. Lila Miller; page 44, copyright © 2000 The Humane Society of the United States; page 54, copyright © 2000 Dr. Thomas Arand; page 58, copyright © 2000 The Humane Society of the United States; page 61, copyright © 2000 The Humane Society of the United States; page 63, copyright © 2000 Roni McFadden; page 66, copyright © 2000 Stephanie Romm; page 68, copyright © 2000 Karol A. Keave; page 78, copyright © 2000 Bill Wagner; page 83, copyright © 2000 The Humane Society of the United States; page 87, copyright © 2000 Patty Dennis; page 96, copyright © 2000 Merlin D. Tuttle; page 99, copyright © 2000 Merlin D. Tuttle; page 101, copyright © 2000 April Ottey; page 106, copyright © 2000 The Marine Mammal Center; page 109, copyright © 2000 The Marine Mammal Center; page 111, copyright © 2000 The Raptor Trust; page 114, copyright © 2000 The Raptor Trust; page 116, copyright © 2000 Jim Sirch; page 121, copyright © 2000 Dave Stauffer; page 134, copyright © 2000 Talbot Productions; page 137, copyright © 1989 Bob Talbot; page 139, copyright © 2000 Environmental Media Corporation; page 144, copyright © 2000 Hope Ryden; page 148, copyright © 2000 Julie Zickefoose; page 151, copyright © 2000 Julie Zickefoose; page 153, copyright © 2000 Living Music Foundation; page 162, copyright © 2000 Vicki Grayland; page 166, copyright © 2000 The Humane Society of the United States; page 170, copyright © 2000 Christine Cook; page 173, copyright © 2000 Christine Cook; page 175, copyright © 2000 Carol Tracy; page 180, copyright © 2000 The Humane Society of the United States.

All rights reserved. No part of this book may be reproduced, stored in a retrieval system, or transmitted in any form or by any means, electronic, mechanical, photocopying, recording, or otherwise, without the prior written permission of the publisher.

Library of Congress Cataloging-in-Publication Data

The Humane Society of the United States
    Careers with animals / The Humane Society of the United States; written by Willow Ann Sirch.
        p. cm.
    Includes bibliographical references and index.
    Summary: Describes various careers dealing with animals and the education and training necessary for such jobs as veterinarian, pet trainer, wildlife rehabilatator, humane investigator, photographer, and naturalist.
    ISBN 1-55591-408-X (alk. paper)
    1. Animal welfare—Vocational guidance—United States—Juvenile literature. 2. Animal shelters—Vocational guidance—United States—Juvenile literature. 3. Wildlife conservation—Vocational guidance—United States—Juvenile literature. 4. Veterinary medicine—Vocational guidance—United States—Juvenile literature. 5. Photography of animals—Vocational guidance—United States—Juvenile literature. [1. Animal welfare—Vocational guidance. 2. Veterinary medicine—Vocational guidance. 3. Wildlife conservation—Vocational guidance. 4. Photography of animals—Vocational guidance. 5. Vocational guidance.] I. Humane Society of the United States. II. Title.

HV4764.S52 2000
636.08'32'02373—dc21   99–086735

Printed in the United States of America
0 9 8 7 6 5 4 3 2 1

Cover illustration and book design: Ann W. Douden, Boulder, Colorado

Fulcrum Publishing
16100 Table Mountain Parkway, Suite 300
Golden, Colorado 80403
(800) 992-2908 or (303) 277-1623
www.fulcrum-resources.com

Contents

Introduction 1

part one—Careers at Animal Shelters 5

    Chapter 1—Humane Society Director: Pamela Burns,
        Hawaiian Humane Society 12

    Chapter 2—Animal Control Agency Director: Belinda Lewis,
        Fort Wayne Animal Control 17

    Chapter 3—Animal Control/Humane Officer: Kathryn Destreza,
        Louisiana SPCA 21

    Chapter 4—Humane Investigator: David Garcia, Houston SPCA 25

    Chapter 5—Humane Educator: Barbara Scanlon, Marshall County Animal
        Rescue League, West Virginia 30

    Chapter 6—Large Animal Shelter Director: Earlene Cole,
        Humane Society of Missouri 35

    Chapter 7—Animal Shelter Veterinarian: Dr. Lila Miller, ASPCA ... 39

    Chapter 8—Disaster Relief Specialist: Laura Bevan, The Humane Society
        of the United States 44

part two—Careers in Veterinary Medicine 49

    Chapter 9—Small Animal Veterinarian: Dr. Thomas Arand 54

    Chapter 10—Wildlife Veterinarian: Dr. Patrice Klein, HSUS-WRTC .. 58

    Chapter 11—Large Animal Veterinarian: Dr. Paul Michelsen 63

    Chapter 12—Veterinary Technician: Ron Sampson 68

part three—Careers Working with Pets 73

    Chapter 13—Obedience Trainer: Barbara Long, Paw in Hand 78

    Chapter 14—Pet-Sitter: Donna Pease, Tendercare Pet-Sitting 83

Chapter 15—Pet Taxi Driver: Larry Reilly, Pet Taxi 87

part four—Careers Working with Wildlife 91

Chapter 16—Wildlife Biologist: Dr. Merlin Tuttle, Bat Conservation
International 96

Chapter 17—Animal Communication Specialist: Dr. Roger Fouts and
Deborah Fouts, Friends of Washoe 101

Chapter 18—Marine Mammal Stranding Specialist: Dawn Smith,
The Marine Mammal Center 106

Chapter 19—Wildlife Rehabilitator: Dr. Len Soucy, The Raptor Trust 111

Chapter 20—Naturalist: Lori Paradis Brant, The Connecticut Audubon Society . . 116

Chapter 21—Wildlife Refuge Manager: Hope Sawyer Buyukmihci,
Unexpected Wildlife Refuge 121

part five—Careers in the Arts 127

Chapter 22—Photographer: Bob Talbot 134

Chapter 23—Video Producer: Bill Pendergraft, Environmental Media
Corporation 139

Chapter 24—Writer: Hope Ryden 144

Chapter 25—Artist: Julie Zickefoose 148

Chapter 26—Musician: Paul Winter 153

part six—Specialty Careers 157

Chapter 27—Lawyer: Scott Beckstead 162

Chapter 28—Lobbyist: Ann Church, The Humane Society of the United States . . 166

Chapter 29—Humane Landscape Designer: Christine Cook, Mossaics 170

Chapter 30—Classroom Teacher: Carol Tracy 175

Chapter 31—HSUS's Executive Officer: Patricia Forkan, The Humane
Society of the United States 180

Index 184

Introduction

Are animals an important part of your life? Can you lose yourself in activities like watching wild birds, walking your dog or playing with your cat? Are you one of those people who is filled with wonder at the way animals live, think and respond? Maybe you have even thought you might like to spend your life working with animals—not in a job that merely puts animals to use, but in one that actively helps animals. If so, you've come to the right place. This book was designed with you in mind.

Many Choices

At one time, people who wanted to work with animals were limited in what they could do. Most went into animal shelter jobs or veterinary medicine. Today the options within these two areas have greatly increased, and many additional opportunities have become available.

This book was developed to help you identify some of the choices open to people who love animals and want to make them a part of their everyday work life. As you read about the different people in this book who have chosen to work with animals, you may even come up with new ideas of your own for animal-related careers. This is an exciting time to be thinking about and exploring different career paths. The world of work is changing faster than ever before, and new job possibilities that bring people and animals together are always just around the corner.

Building Career Awareness

Understanding the world of work and planning for an animal-related career are processes that take time. They begin with a serious look at your interests, likes and dislikes and involve developing your knowledge, experience and abilities. Even if you are a long way from choosing a career, there is plenty you can do to improve your career awareness. Reading this book and following some of the suggestions for further exploration included in each chapter are a good start.

You might also think about the animal-related careers you find in real life, on television or in other books you read. Try creating a network of relatives, family friends and people in your community who work to help animals. Your local telephone directory can help you identify people, organizations and businesses that have the welfare of animals at heart. Humane agencies and professional organizations can provide you with names of people to contact for information about necessary education, skills and training. And, advertisements in animal-related magazines can lead you to additional resources.

The Internet is another good resource for exploring animal-related jobs. You can learn more about humane agencies, animal welfare organizations and animal-related businesses by visiting their websites. You can also access information about colleges, universities and technical schools that can help you prepare for a job working with animals.

Finding ways to practice your own entrepreneurial skills can be helpful in your effort to learn more about animal-related work and workplaces. Many of today's jobs require good business skills. Even nonprofit groups must use their time and money wisely. Understanding the basics of how business operates is important to an animal-related career, whether you decide to run your own business, work for someone else's or pursue a job at a humane organization.

Your career choice should be based on what you love to do, your special talents and your ability to master any needed skills. Exploring different career options is well worth your effort, because it will help guide you in facing one of the most important decisions you will ever make—choosing your life's work.

Questions to Explore

How can you know if working with animals will be right for you? Start by taking stock of yourself and your feelings. Do you care deeply about the welfare of animals? Are you willing to live on what may be a modest income? Are you prepared for long hours and often stressful situations? Can you deal with being misunderstood by people who do not share your love of animals?

Additional questions will help you decide what specific area of animal-related work might be right for you. Do you want to work directly with animals—that is, feed and care for them? Or would you be content simply to know that your efforts are helping animals—even those you may never see? Do you like to work with people? Working with animals often involves a human element, from the distraught pet owner to the concerned citizen who takes in a stray dog or rescues an injured baby bird.

Some jobs require many years of education and special skills. Others demand great physical strength and energy. Still others require the basic skills you are developing in school every day—writing, speaking and studying. A job working with animals can be challenging, difficult and tiring. But for someone who truly cares about animals, there may be no greater reward.

part one
Careers at Animal Shelters

When animals are in trouble, often the only place they can receive help is at an animal shelter. In the United States, shelters take in millions of animals each year. In addition to dogs, cats and other companion animals, many animal shelters care for wildlife and farm animals.

Animal shelters provide lost, unwanted and abandoned animals with a temporary home. They treat sick animals. They try to locate the owners of lost pets. When owners cannot be found, animal shelters make every effort to find new homes for the pets in their care. They also teach the public about the needs of animals and how to care for them properly. Their work helps animals and people alike.

Who Runs Animal Shelters

Some animal shelters are run by nonprofit organizations. A humane society is an example. The money to run such a shelter does not come from the city or state government, but from people in the community. Other shelters are run by local government departments. Such a shelter might be called an animal care and control agency. The money to run this type of shelter usually comes from taxes paid by people who live in the city or town that the shelter serves.

Who Works at Animal Shelters

It takes many people in different jobs to keep an animal shelter running smoothly. Some of the workers at animal shelters are humane investigators, managers, secretaries, animal care attendants, veterinarians, veterinary technicians and humane educators. Most shelters also rely on volunteers.

The pay at animal shelters varies depending on location, the size of the shelter and the difficulty of the duties involved. Some jobs require plenty of hands-on contact with animals. Others involve little direct contact with animals. For instance, a shelter director sees animals and helps solve their problems daily, but the hands-on work of feeding and caring for the animals is usually done by others.

Managing an Animal Shelter

There are many educational paths that can lead to work in an animal shelter. Some animal shelter directors come from jobs as managers in other professions. Others work their way up to the position of director from shelter jobs that require less education or experience.

To run a shelter, you need good leadership skills and good business skills. Depending on the shelter, you may need an undergraduate degree to work as a manager or director, as well as special training in law enforcement. It can be helpful to have an advanced degree in business management or animal science. Undergraduate courses in business, science, speech, writing, math and education are also helpful. Today some colleges and universities are developing advanced degrees that will be important for those who choose to become animal shelter directors in the future.

Working with Animals and Law Enforcement

The work of the humane officer or animal care and control officer is vital to any animal shelter. Different towns and cities have different names for this job. A person might be called a humane officer in one place and an animal care and control officer or animal warden in another. In any case, the work is similar. It involves responding to calls about animals who have been injured or neglected, bringing animals back to the shelter, and enforcing animal control or anti-cruelty laws, and it sometimes involves rescuing animals.

A good humane officer needs courage, strength and patience, and he or she needs to understand the "body language" of animals. Good communication skills, an understanding of animal control laws, and an ability to make sound judgments quickly are important. This job often calls for physical strength and persistence. A person in this job must be able to handle and control large animals who may be hurt or frightened. However, the ability to calm an animal through gentle speech and kindness is just as important. A general high school education is usually enough to begin working at this job.

Like the humane officer, the humane investigator also responds to calls about animals who have been injured or neglected. This career sometimes involves a certain amount of detective work, as its duties include investigating people who may have harmed animals and stopping any abuse. The humane investigator may start out as a humane officer or other animal shelter worker. A person in this career must have good communication skills, including an ability to deal with the public in a positive, upbeat manner. The humane investigator must be experienced in handling and controlling animals and needs training in law enforcement and investigation procedures. Because presenting evidence is vital to this job, good writing and investigative skills are also important.

Teaching People About Animals

Some people start out at animal shelters as humane educators. They may come to this career from working as a classroom teacher or as a teacher's aide. An undergraduate degree and courses in education are helpful in this job. A humane educator needs to have the qualities of a good teacher—like patience and the ability to communicate effectively—and also needs to know a great deal about animals. The job of the humane educator is not a paid position at every animal shelter, and its responsibilities may be handled part-time by a staff member who has other duties as well.

The job of the humane educator is to prevent animal suffering by teaching people about the needs of animals. People who work at animal shelters say that most of the suffering that animals experience is caused by people's ignorance rather than by deliberate cruelty. A person in this career should be comfortable speaking to groups of people of all ages.

Helping Large Animals

In addition to caring for small animals, some shelters care for large animals like horses, cows, sheep or llamas. They may arrange for large animals to receive foster care at nearby farms or stables. Or they may have a special place for providing a temporary home to large animals who are lost, injured, abandoned or sick. Experience with large animals is important for this job. Other requirements include physical strength and fitness, a knowledge of the particular needs of large animals, and good communication skills. For this line of work, courses in animal science and husbandry are especially helpful. Experience can come from working or volunteering at a farm, stable or other place where large animals are housed.

Medical Careers at Animal Shelters

Some animal shelters have a full- or part-time veterinarian on staff. Some also employ veterinary technicians. Shelter staff who are trained in animal medicine are responsible for treating sick or injured animals and making sure that animals put up for adoption are healthy. Veterinarians must train rigorously for many years. In addition to attending college and veterinary medical school, a veterinarian must take a series of tests to become certified before practicing animal medicine. Veterinary staff at animal shelters usually make less money than those who work in private practice.

The real reward of this job is helping homeless animals, many of whom may never have received medical care before—and many of whose lives would otherwise be lost.

Disaster Relief for Animals

Some jobs related to animal shelter work, such as the position of the disaster relief specialist, are not found at all shelters. The work of managing animals in an emergency might be handled by someone with a different title—the chief investigator or operations director, for instance. The disaster relief specialist featured in Chapter 8 helps animal shelters when a disaster strikes. Requirements for this career include training in emergency management and a thorough knowledge of the care, handling and control of stray and injured animals. People usually come to this kind of work from other animal protection jobs or from the field of emergency management.

Your Local Animal Shelter—A Great Resource

The best place to learn more about working in an animal shelter is right at hand. Talk to the people who work at a shelter near you. Whether it goes by the name of humane society, animal care and control agency, SPCA (Society for the Prevention of Cruelty to Animals) or some other humane organization title, you will learn a lot by talking to the people who work there. And guess what? Many of them will be happy to tell you about what they do and why they do it.

Decide which kinds of jobs most interest you. Make a telephone call to your local animal shelter and ask if someone who works in one of those positions will speak to you in person or on the telephone. Be flexible. The person you want to talk to may be busy, so you may need to arrange your discussion to fit his or her schedule. But don't be shy about asking for the opportunity. And, if the person you want to speak to cannot help you, don't give up. Try asking someone in another position.

You might also want to consider volunteering at your local shelter. The experience might help you decide whether a career working with animals is right for you.

Many shelters offer a junior volunteer program for young people in which you may feed, handle and exercise animals brought to the shelter. Even if you decide that working at an animal shelter is not right for you, you will learn a lot about yourself and how you work with others. These are important things to know, whatever career you decide upon.

Choosing Your Career

Discovering the job that is right for you is an exciting adventure. It is also one of the most important things you will ever do. Even if you are not yet old enough to set out on your career, it's never too early to start thinking about it. If you love animals, working at an animal shelter might be right for you, but how can you be sure? Here are some suggestions to get you started in exploring what your future career will be.

Start by asking yourself some questions—and be honest with yourself about the answers. For instance, are you comfortable doing what you believe is right—even when others might not understand your actions? Do you want to work with animals—even when they are sick, scared or hurt? Nearly everyone who works at an animal shelter educates people about animals at some point in their work. Are you comfortable teaching others? If you answered yes to all these questions, keep working to pinpoint your interests in a career at an animal shelter.

Your Favorite Subject

You can also focus on animals at school. Choose an animal-related topic for your next writing assignment. Start an afterschool animal awareness club. Or look into participating in an animal-related Explorers' Post through a Boy Scout office in your area. (Explorers' Posts give young people an opportunity to try out different career opportunities, and both boys and girls may participate.) With some thought, you will come up with other ways to work your favorite subject into your schoolwork and extracurricular activities.

A career working with animals is one of the most rewarding you can have. But it takes time to find the career that is right for you. Be open to new experiences. Follow your dreams. The perfect career is waiting just around the corner.

chapter one
HUMANE SOCIETY DIRECTOR

© PAMELA BURNS

As the director of the Hawaiian Humane Society, Pamela Burns works hard to help animals.

America is filled with people who love animals. We say that dogs are "man's best friend," and plenty of people agree about that. In the United States alone, about fifty-eight million dogs today are somebody's pet. For even more people, cats are the pet of choice—about sixty-six million of them find homes with American families.

We love our pets. As a nation, we spend millions of dollars every year on their medical care, food and even toys to amuse them. So why is there a need for humane societies?

"Not everyone knows how to treat animals properly or take care of them," says Pamela Burns, president and director of the Hawaiian Humane Society. "Most of the animals who come to us are not the victims of deliberate cruelty. They are the victims of ignorance."

Pam is responsible for managing this large humane society and animal shelter in Honolulu. A humane society is usually a privately run organization. This means that the money used to run it comes from its members. The Hawaiian Humane Society is also responsible for animal care and control. It receives some money from the city to rescue animals and handle the problems that people encounter.

"At the Hawaiian Humane Society," says Pam, "we provide food and care for thousands of lost, homeless and abandoned animals every year. We reunite lost pets with their owners. We solve animal problems so animals can stay with their owners. We also teach people how to be good neighbors and pet owners. We have a humane education program that goes into the schools here. I think the most significant work we do is helping young people develop compassion, respect and responsibility for all living creatures. That, to me, is truly the solution to the problems animals face."

The Hawaiian Humane Society is dedicated to helping all animals—not just dogs and cats, but everything from wild pigs, horses and cattle to birds and fish. "Yes, even fish," says Pam. "The state capitol here had a cracked manmade fishpond. The person in charge was going to let the water drain out of the pond—which would have killed all the fish. The fish were a species called Tilapia." For her efforts to save the fish, Pam was jokingly referred to in the local papers as "The Tilapia Queen." If you want to help animals, you can't give up just because a few people might laugh at you.

Usually, Pam does not work directly with animals. "A lot of my day is spent in meetings," she laughs. "That might not sound very exciting, but people meet because they have problems to solve. Solving those problems can be exciting—especially when the people involved do not agree with one another."

Pam was born and raised in Hawaii. Cats, dogs, myna birds and geese were just some of the creatures on the sugar plantation where she grew up. She also had a horse as a pet. She loved animals and hoped one day to have a career helping them. Like many people, Pam thought the only animal-related job she could get was as a veterinarian. So she worked for an animal hospital in the summer. Then she went to college and found that her best subjects were not biology and chemistry—the kinds of classes you need to become a veterinarian—but social work, psychology and sociology. Pam chose a career in child protection.

For many years Pam worked as a manager in child protection offices. But she continued to work with animals as a volunteer. In time, through her volunteer efforts, she realized that she could put her management skills to work for animals. This led Pam to change her career.

Today Pam loves working as the director of a humane society. "People can come to this kind of work from a wide variety of backgrounds," she says. "It takes good management skills and commitment to animals." What are "management skills"? Knowing how to direct other people to get a job done is one. Being good at working with a wide range of people is another.

"I also look at our community needs. I see which needs are being met and which ones are not. Then I think about how we can better serve the needs of animals and people in our community. Working with others, I come up with ways to address the needs of animals where we live."

Pam is especially proud of the Pet Bereavement program she started. The humane society provides counseling for people whose pets have died. It also offers a program for people who are ill or elderly. By providing pet care volunteers, the humane society enables the ill and elderly to keep their pets. "When you are sick," says Pam, "you need the love and companionship of your pet the most!"

Is there anything Pam does not like about her job? "One of the hardest things is to see the large number of unwanted animals that must be humanely euthanized," she says. Euthanasia is when animals must be killed quickly and painlessly by injection. "Our number-one challenge," says Pam, "is to get people to spay and neuter their pets to prevent unwanted births. There are simply many more pets than there are homes to go around." Making sure that every animal has a good home is important.

That is why the Hawaiian Humane Society focuses on spaying and neutering animals like dogs and cats—and even pet rabbits and guinea pigs.

There are some who might say that Pam is a natural leader. But being a leader, like any other skill, can be learned. As a young person, Pam practiced her leadership skills—perhaps without even realizing it. She taught horseback riding and expanded the horse program at the private school she attended. This gave her a chance to develop confidence. Also, to be able to manage something well, you need to know as much as possible about it. Pam's experiences taught her the importance of being well-informed about all aspects of her job.

What advice does Pam have for young readers who might want to manage a humane society someday? "Always play fair," she says. "Be truthful and honest with others. When you are the leader, you need to have high standards." Clearly, Pam's standards are high. Having a job that she loves, that she is good at, and that helps animals is not just a matter of luck. She made it happen. You can too.

Could You Have a Career as a Humane Society Director?

What do you think? Could a career as a humane society director be the one for you? Get a head start. You don't need to wait until you are old enough to get a job to start thinking about whether this career might be right for you. Here are some ideas you can explore right now:

1. Take a tour of your local animal shelter. You'll learn a lot—not just about animals, but also about yourself. If your local shelter has a junior volunteer program, join it. Volunteering is one of the best ways you can give something to animals and to your community.

2. Interview an animal shelter director or manager as a class project. Prepare your questions ahead of time. Share what you learn with classmates. There may be some aspects of the job that you never thought of before.

3. Practice opportunities to be a leader. Speak up in class, organize a project or start a club that helps animals. Being a leader is never easy, but with practice your leadership skills can only improve.

chapter 2
ANIMAL CONTROL AGENCY DIRECTOR

As the director of the Fort Wayne Department of Animal Care and Control, Belinda Lewis sees to it that animal-related laws are properly enforced within the community.

© BELINDA LEWIS

Animals have problems just like humans. They can hurt themselves or harm people. What kinds of animal problems happen in a community? Perhaps a stray kitten is stuck high on the steel girders of a bridge. Who will rescue him? Perhaps a dangerous animal is running loose. Who will capture her? Or perhaps a circus has come to town and someone has complained that the animals appear to be neglected or sick. Who will investigate?

These are the kinds of decisions that Belinda Lewis must make every day. She is the director of the Fort Wayne Department of Animal Care and Control in Fort Wayne, Indiana. As the director of a large animal control department and shelter, Belinda has a very busy, demanding job. It requires her to know a great deal about animals, animal shelters, law enforcement and her community.

As an animal control agency director, Belinda usually does not work closely with animals. Instead, she directs the work of people. Every day her decisions affect the lives of animals and residents where she lives. "Each morning, I review what the high-risk situations in the community may be," she says. "I decide what must be dealt with first. I ask myself, 'What do we need to do today to make sure that people and pets in the community stay safe? And, what is the order in which we need to do it?'" Like the director of a humane society, Belinda has a career that demands excellent leadership and communication skills, as well as good judgment.

There are many similarities between the work of a humane society and that of an animal control department like the one where Belinda works. Like many humane societies, her department includes an animal shelter that rescues stray and abandoned animals and tries to locate their owners. When the owners cannot be found, the department tries to find new homes for the animals. As part of its work, the Fort Wayne Department of Animal Care and Control also spays and neuters pets. In addition, staff members teach the public about the needs of animals and the proper way to care for them, so fewer animals will suffer because of ignorance.

Are there important differences between the work of a humane society and that of an animal control agency? Belinda thinks so. "In animal control," she explains, "our first goal is public safety. We are a government agency. The city hires us to protect people and animals and to handle animal problems. We protect people from health risks and the dangers that animals can cause. We also protect animals from cruelty and neglect.

"As the director," says Belinda, "it is my job to think of ways to make things better for animals in our community." One of the things no one likes about animal shelter work is that there are more pets than there are homes to go around. "Even if we could keep all the unwanted pets in cages forever," she says, "that would not be fair to the animals. Pets need a loving family. Part of my job is to come up with different ideas and programs to get people to spay and neuter their pets. That way, there will be fewer pets without homes."

Belinda started out as the director of a small humane society, where she enjoyed helping animals and running a businesslike organization. While working there, Belinda experienced some of the differences between a humane society and a government animal control agency. "For one thing," says Belinda, "I found that the public often thought of animal control agencies in a bad way—as dog pounds. I wanted to change that negative image. I liked the fact that the animal control department had more power to enforce laws protecting animals and people."

In time, Belinda moved on to her current job in animal control. "As the director of a public safety department," she says, "I feel that I have more opportunity to help animals. Sometimes, as a humane society director, I felt that my hands were tied. Today, I can do more about the problems I see." Belinda is a graduate of the local police academy and a commissioned police officer. Ensuring that animal protection laws are enforced plays an important role in her work.

"My work helps animals and people in many ways," says Belinda. "It helps make a safer community for animals to live in. Also, through our education programs, we teach the public about the needs of animals, how to treat them humanely and how to follow laws about animals where we live."

Although most of her work does not involve direct contact with animals, helping them is still what provides Belinda with her favorite moments on the job. "I love to see a pet go to a good home," she says. "I love a good rescue. And it makes me feel great when we are able to resolve a problem with a positive result for both people and animals."

Perhaps the most difficult part of Belinda's job is that she continues to see many of the same problems again and again. People still turn over their animals to the shelter for reasons that indicate they should not have owned a pet in the first place. Sadly, these same people often turn around and get another pet. Although this can be very frustrating, Belinda maintains a positive attitude toward her work. "This does not mean we are not having an impact," she says. "It is just that sometimes it is hard to see the impact that we have on a daily basis."

It might sound glamorous to do work that protects animals. It can also be appealing to think of spending your days telling other people what to do. Is the job really that easy? Think again. Being the director of an animal care and control department takes hard work, patience and persistence. But if you are as dedicated as Belinda Lewis is, it can also be a very rewarding career.

Could You Have a Career as an
Animal Control Agency Director?

Could a career as an animal control agency director be right for you? Here are some suggestions to help you answer this question:

1. Contact your local law enforcement department. Find out about animal laws where you live and who enforces them.

2. Talk to others about the need to observe animal laws in your community.

3. Interview the director of a local animal control agency or other city department. Find out what it's like to be in charge.

4. Take a bold step: Practice taking on new responsibility at home, at school or in an afterschool group.

chapter 3
ANIMAL CONTROL/HUMANE OFFICER

At the Louisiana Society for the Protection of Animals, Humane Officer Kathryn Destreza has her hands full with two rescued kittens.

The puppy had escaped from his owner's yard earlier in the day. He was enjoying himself. He found all the strange sights and smells very exciting. When he caught sight of an open drainpipe, he could not help wondering what was inside. He put his little head in to get a good look. That was when he got into trouble. His head became lodged in the drainpipe. Fortunately, a neighbor found the puppy and called the Louisiana Society for the Protection of Animals (LASPCA). That was when Kathryn Destreza took charge. Kathryn is a humane officer (also known as an animal control officer) for the LASPCA, which runs an animal shelter in New Orleans.

"First, I tried to pull the puppy out of the drainpipe," Kathryn explains. "But that did not work. He was really stuck. Finally, I got someone to cut off the end of the drainpipe. Then I took everything—puppy and pipe together—back to the animal shelter. That way, I could get our veterinarian to help. We put grease on the puppy's head. It was like trying to get a ring off your finger. The grease made the ring of pipe slip right off. In the end, the puppy was fine."

During a typical day, a humane officer answers many calls. Calls come from all kinds of people in all kinds of places. An office worker might call about a sick or injured cat seen in an alley. A teacher might call about a homeless dog who keeps coming into the school yard. A home owner might call about a raccoon who is active during the day and exhibiting other strange behavior.

Kathryn responds to a call by going to the place where the animal was last seen and trying to help. She has a special truck made just for picking up animals. It has a section for the animals, with separate cages so they can't hurt themselves, the driver, or one another. Kathryn often takes her own dog with her when she goes out on a call. As you might have guessed, her dog—a little mixed-breed Corgie—came from the shelter.

"I've answered many different kinds of calls," Kathryn explains. "I've pulled dogs out of canals, gotten cats out of trees and rescued animals that were high up on the big steel beams of bridges. When I first came to work here, I did not realize all the trouble animals can get into," she says. "I never would have guessed."

A humane officer's work can be dangerous. Often, a humane officer is called upon to help the local police. When you watch police shows on television, the arrests usually go pretty smoothly. That's not always true in real life. When the police go to a residence to arrest someone or search their property, there may be a growling dog waiting for them. The suspect may have a dog to keep everyone (including the police) away. How to keep the dog from hurting anyone? That is the humane officer's job—to make sure the police can do their work safely. If there is no one to care for the dog afterward, the humane officer takes the dog to the shelter.

Many humane officers like the variety of their job. No day is ever quite the same as another. People who are flexible and like to think on their feet find this kind of job very appealing. Every call is different, and so is every animal who needs help.

What are some of the challenges that come with this kind of work? "People who ignore suffering, who don't want to get involved, are hard to deal with," says Kathryn. "Working with them is probably the hardest part of my job." Speaking to people calmly and firmly—making them understand—is part of every humane officer's work.

Sometimes people misunderstand the work of the humane officer. They may not like being told what to do—even when they are breaking the law. They may see the humane officer as someone who is there not to help animals, but to cause trouble. One of the challenges of being a humane officer is helping these people understand that laws to protect animals are important, that animals need care and sometimes need help. Trying to get people to change their behavior toward animals is not always easy. A humane officer must be able to defuse a tense situation before it gets out of control. He or she must be patient, calm and firm. Working with the public can be difficult, yet it is also very rewarding. "I like that my job helps both animals and people," says Kathryn. "As an officer of the SPCA, I enforce laws that protect animals. By enforcing these laws and educating people, I help people as well."

Rescuing animals, enforcing the law and teaching are all part of the work of the humane officer. Of these, Kathryn says that she likes teaching best. "I enjoy educating the public about how to care for animals. I especially like to talk to children," she explains. "I still get surprised at the number of people who don't realize that pets need more than just food and water." Kathryn teaches adults and children alike about the things that pets need—food, water, shelter, yearly checkups, spaying or neutering, daily exercise, grooming and attention.

What message does Kathryn have for readers interested in work as a humane officer? She believes that young people who want to help animals can start right now by talking to other people about the importance of spaying and neutering pets. "It's our biggest problem," says Kathryn. "And the answer is so simple. You will find that sometimes people are more willing to listen to children. You might be surprised at the good you can do just by talking to others about what animals need." Like Humane Officer Kathryn Destreza, you too can help animals.

Could You Have a Career as a Humane Officer?

Are you interested in law enforcement? Do you like thinking on your feet? Are you the kind of person who can defuse a tense situation before it gets out of control? If so, a career as a humane officer might be right for you. Here are some suggestions for further exploration:

1. Contact your local humane society and investigate joining a junior volunteer program.

2. Interview a humane officer who works at your local humane society or animal control agency. Or, ask your teacher if you can invite a humane officer to speak to your class at school.

3. Know what to do if you see an animal in trouble: Don't try to help the animal yourself. Take note of where the animal is and what the animal looks like, then call your local humane society or animal control agency. If you are with a friend, have that person watch the animal while you make the call.

chapter 4
HUMANE INVESTIGATOR

As chief investigator for the Houston Society for the Protection of Animals, David Garcia leads a highly trained investigative team.

© DAVID GARCIA

A call has come into the animal shelter. The voice of the woman on the other end of the line sounds nervous. She says that a family is neglecting their three horses. The animals are scrawny and underfed. One of them has an injured hoof. The woman will not give her name. She is afraid of what the family might do if they discover she has complained about them.

It's a tricky situation. Someone needs to find out what is happening, get help for the animals if they need it, and make sure the owners stop breaking the law. It's a job for the humane investigator.

Many animal shelters employ humane investigators to look into complaints about people who may be hurting animals. The humane investigator gives citations (or warnings) to people who break the law by harming animals. If the person does not stop willingly, the humane investigator may need to gather evidence against that person so he or she can be taken to court and forced to stop. Sometimes this is the only way to help animals that are being abused.

As chief investigator for the Houston Society for the Protection of Animals in Houston, Texas, David Garcia leads a highly trained investigative team. He works with law enforcement officers throughout the state of Texas. He also trains others to become humane investigators.

David starts each morning by reading any new reports and messages. Then he schedules his work for the day. "You never know what assignment you will be working on in this job," he says. "I have to be very flexible."

A humane investigator spends lots of time traveling from one place to another—usually by car—responding to calls that have already come in. In addition, the humane investigator may receive emergency calls during the day from the humane society dispatcher. When this happens, the investigator must usually respond immediately, breaking in on what he or she has planned for the day.

The most important part of a humane investigator's work is to educate people. The humane investigator teaches people how to care for their animals in a manner that is acceptable to their community and the court system. He or she must be firm, but must also remain calm. As David explains, "I don't get angry. My job is to enforce the law, not punish the offender. That is the job of the court if it comes to that."

When David encounters a suspect, he explains to that person what he or she must do to avoid any further involvement with the law. If the suspect follows David's instructions, and the problem is solved, the matter ends there. If the person fails to meet the requirements of the law, David sees to it that the offender is taken to court. "My team of humane investigators is successful because we do not go about our work in a confrontational way," he says. "We give the suspect a chance to correct the problem. If the problem is not corrected, we prepare the evidence and take it to the prosecuting attorney for our district."

If the district attorney agrees, the matter is brought before a judge, who decides whether a law has been broken and determines an appropriate punishment. The punishment for most cases is a fine and/or community service—often at an animal shelter. In some cases, an offender's animals are taken away and the individual may no longer keep animals as long as he or she lives within the state.

What are the tools of David's trade? "I travel in a four-wheel-drive vehicle," he explains. "I have radio contact with the animal shelter at all times. In the back of the vehicle, I keep a kennel [a crate with a handle for carrying animals] and special gloves that keep me from being bitten by animals who are scared or injured. I also have nets, a flashlight, plastic bags for gathering evidence, insect repellent, rubber boots to help me get through mud or water, binoculars, a 35mm camera with telephoto lens, a video camera, clipboard, and maps for getting around."

David also keeps blank warrants with him, which he can fill out and get an authorized signature promptly in case he needs to go onto someone's property and investigate a complaint. Normally, he can only investigate what he can see from public land (that is, from the road that passes the suspect's house). If what he sees gives him reason to think that a crime against an animal has been committed, he can get a warrant and go onto the property. David also keeps another type of form with him, called a witness affidavit. If there is a witness to a crime involving an animal, the witness can write what he or she saw on the affidavit, which then becomes part of the evidence against the suspect.

A strong love of animals is important in this challenging and sometimes dangerous career. David comes to his love of animals, in part, through his cultural heritage as a Native American. "I am a member of the Tohono O'Odham nation," he says. "We respect all life. We believe that all life is in a kind of balance. According to our tradition, whenever an animal or human is injured or killed, it throws off that natural balance within our universe, our way of life. Within our tribe, we have people we call 'singers,' who sing to the gods to bring the universe back into balance. I was taught to respect these traditional beliefs regarding animals at a very early age."

Organization and attention to detail are skills that a humane investigator needs every day in his or her work. Good writing skills are also very important. Just like a reporter, the humane investigator needs to focus on the five Ws and one H: Who, What, Where, When, Why and How.

And just like a police detective, the humane investigator needs to know how to conduct an investigation—a responsibility that involves collecting and preserving evidence, "running" license plates (matching a license plate number with a car's owner), determining who owns a piece of property (by looking up tax records, for instance) and so on. If the humane investigator cannot show the exact circumstances under which a crime was committed, a judge cannot be sure that things happened the way the investigator says they did.

Excellent investigative skills, dedication to animals and great people skills—that's what it takes to succeed as a humane investigator. If you have a strong desire to help animals, want to work in law enforcement and don't give up when the going gets tough, you might one day find yourself working in this challenging and rewarding career.

Could You Have a Career as a Humane Investigator?

Would you have the patience to observe closely, look up information carefully and follow up on details? These are some of the skills that a good humane investigator needs. Here are some ideas to help you decide whether this career might be right for you:

1. Practice your writing skills. Write a report and be sure to include the five Ws and one H—just like a humane investigator does.

2. Learn more about resolving conflicts. The next time you find yourself in a conflict, try explaining your views to others in a nonconfrontational way.

3. Interview a humane investigator at your local animal shelter.

4. Find out about animal laws in your community by calling your local animal shelter or law enforcement agency. Share what you learn with your classmates.

chapter 5
HUMANE EDUCATOR

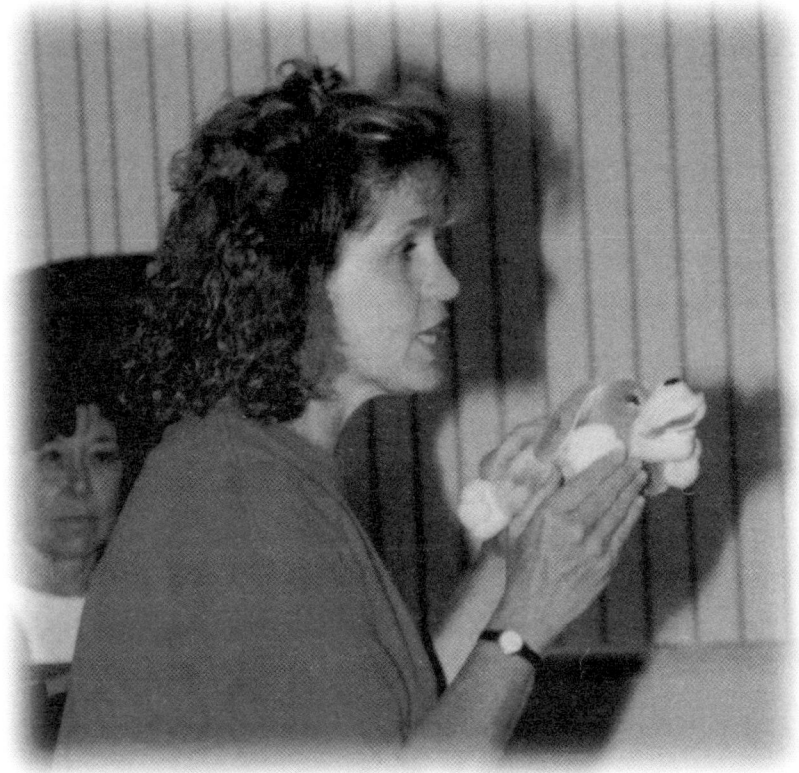

Humane educator Barbara Scanlon helps children understand what it means to treat animals humanely.

It's late in the afternoon. Your class has just finished a long math test. Everyone's brain is drained. Then your teacher says you are about to have a visitor—a humane educator. Everybody perks right up. Will we see some neat animals? you wonder.

When he arrives, however, the humane educator does not have any animals with him. Instead, he sets an empty cage on a desk at the front of the room. He asks the class to guess why the cage is empty. No one knows. The cage is empty, he says, because he is going to talk about wild animals—and a wild animal should never be kept in a cage as a pet. Of course, you probably knew that already, but the humane educator has just educated the rest of your class.

People who work at animal shelters would like to see all animals treated humanely. In addition to the work of rescuing animals and trying to find homes for them, many animal shelters focus on humane education. Those shelters hire a humane educator to teach adults as well as children what it means to be humane.

Barbara Scanlon is the humane educator for the Marshall County Animal Rescue League in West Virginia. She is a dynamic teacher—a "people person" who enjoys working with children and adults. Barbara believes that it is especially important to help students understand the need for kindness.

Just what is humane education? It is not the same as teaching facts about animals. It is about helping others feel compassion, respect and responsibility toward animals. "The goal of the humane educator," says Barbara, "is to help people appreciate what animals experience. From that, people can learn to change their behavior so that their treatment of animals is humane." Like Barbara, most humane educators agree that teaching young children to be kind to animals is a great way to help them develop values of kindness toward people.

Humane educators teach children and adults about the needs of pets—food, water, shelter, exercise, medical care, spaying or neutering, grooming and love. They teach children especially how to stay safe around pets. Not touching stray animals or petting dogs when they are eating or protecting something can be among the humane educator's most important lessons.

Humane educators also teach about wild animals. "Sometimes a child does not understand why it is better to watch a frog in the wild than to catch and keep a frog in a jar in their room," says Barbara. She could approach the lessons she teaches by simply telling her students not to do this or that. "Instead," she says, "I try to help kids appreciate what the animals might be feeling. I want them to come to a decision on their own about what it means to treat animals humanely."

One technique used by many humane educators is to help people relate how we treat animals to how we treat people. "If I am teaching about a misunderstood animal, like a snake or spider," Barbara explains, "I might discuss some of the unusual abilities of the animal and tell how that animal plays a role in its habitat. Then I talk about how people all have special talents too—even though those talents may seem hidden at first. If I were talking to students, I might get them to tell about a time when they felt misunderstood. It is very rewarding when you see children begin to get the message about respecting others—both animals and people."

Barbara sometimes teaches at schools in Marshall County. Other times she teaches family groups at the animal shelter. Through the humane society, Barbara also provides copies of *KIND News* to schools. This publication for elementary classrooms features fun articles about animals and the environment. It is published by the National Association for Humane and Environmental Education.

Many humane educators agree that it is important to share humane education lessons with classroom teachers. That way, teachers can continue the work the humane educator has begun. Each year, Barbara organizes a graduate-level course for teachers through West Virginia University. Her course is very popular. It features speakers from animal protection and educational organizations around the country. In addition to lessons, Barbara provides educational materials and tips on helping students develop values of kindness toward animals and people. Throughout the school year, Barbara stays in touch with the teachers who take her course. She provides them with additional educational handouts for their students as well as classroom posters and other teaching materials.

Humane educators can be found at both small and large animal shelters. They may work full-time or they may divide their time between other jobs at the shelter and teaching humane education. At some shelters the work of the humane educator is done by a volunteer. More and more shelters, however, are hiring full-time humane educators because they recognize that educating the public can reduce the number of stray, abandoned and unneutered pets they encounter each year.

Most humane educators have training in the field of education. Often they are former classroom teachers. Large animal shelters may have a humane education department with a staff of humane educators led by a humane education director. Qualifications to become a humane education director are beyond those of the humane educator, and can include courses in management, writing, communications and public speaking. Like most teachers, humane educators seldom see the effects of their work right away. Yet their influence can have a very important effect. Some people who work in animal shelters say that they first became interested in their careers through a humane educator who spoke to them when they were students.

What advice does Barbara have for young people interested in humane education? "Don't be afraid to share your concern for animals with others," she says. "Just talking about how animals should be treated is a kind of teaching. It is not easy to be kind, caring and sensitive. It is probably harder to do that as a child than as an adult because other children may make fun of you. But having those feelings is something to be proud of. If you stick to your feelings, you can feel good about yourself. You can feel good about helping others see that kindness to animals is the way to go."

Could You Have a Career as a Humane Educator?

Want to work as a humane educator? It's not enough just to be an "animal person." You need to be a "people person" too. Here are some ideas to help you decide whether a career as a humane educator might be right for you:

1. Talk to your favorite teacher about what skills are needed to be an educator. Ask your teacher to give you some mini–teaching opportunities in class. See how you like being at the head of the class. Practice talking in front of a group. For your next speaking assignment, choose an animal topic and test your skills at educating your classmates about animal needs.

2. Talk to the humane educator at a local animal shelter. Ask what he or she likes most and least about the job.

3. Check out *KIND News*, a great resource for teaching humane education. As a class project, subscribe to *KIND News* on behalf of classrooms of younger students at your school. To find out more, write to *KIND News*, P.O. Box 362, East Haddam, CT 06423, or visit their website at http://www.nahee.org/.

chapter 6
LARGE ANIMAL SHELTER DIRECTOR

Director Earlene Cole makes friends with Pegasus the goat, a new arrival at the Humane Society of Missouri's Large Animal Rehabilitation Center.

© EARLENE COLE

Rambo, a little gray pygmy goat, was hungry and tired. He had been brought to the city in a truck and unloaded at the farmer's market along with all the other goats for sale. With a goat's cleverness, he had slipped out of his lead rope. Now he was wandering down an alley in search of food.

A car drove into the alley. Startled, Rambo turned and ran. The next thing he knew, he was in the middle of a busy street. There were cars all around him. Rambo was terrified. "Hey!" cried one driver. "What's a goat doing in the middle of the road? Somebody had better do something about it!"

Rambo was lucky. Someone called the Humane Society of Missouri. One of their investigators came to the scene, picked him up and took him to the humane society's Large Animal Rehabilitation Center (LARC), run by Earlene Cole. Earlene made sure

Rambo received food, water, vaccinations, medicine and a safe place to stay. Before long, Rambo was adopted. He found a great home with a family who owned a farm outside the city. When they saw him, they knew he would be the perfect playmate for the goat they already had.

What kinds of animals come to mind when you think of an animal shelter? Dogs, cats and maybe a guinea pig or rabbit? These are the kinds of animals that most often find their way inside shelter doors. Some animal shelters, however, have a place for sheltering large animals as well. Such a shelter may take in horses, ponies, cows, burros, goats, sheep, pot-bellied pigs and even an occasional llama.

At the LARC, Earlene Cole directs assistants and works with outside help—veterinarians, blacksmiths and trainers. She also performs much of the hands-on work with the animals. The LARC is actually a farm that covers 165 acres. It includes a large, grassy pasture and fourteen paddocks (fenced-in areas that are smaller than a pasture yet larger than a pen). There are four barns. Three are divided into stalls and areas where sick animals can be kept apart until they are well. The other barn is for storing feed and equipment. Male and female animals are kept in separate places to prevent unwanted babies.

What kinds of chores need to be done at a large animal shelter? Feeding and watering all the animals in the barns and pastures is one job. Some animals may require up to three meals a day. Cleaning stalls and replacing dirty straw with clean bedding are other daily tasks. Most animals need to be exercised, and some require medicine or other special care. In addition, fields need to be mowed, fences need to be mended and equipment needs to be maintained. The animal shelter should look nice, not just for the animals, but also for the people come here to adopt animals. Unless they are being held in a legal case, all the animals at a large animal shelter are usually up for adoption. There are other chores as well. For example, horses are weighed each week at the LARC. "Some have to be weighed every day," says Earlene, "if we are trying to help them gain weight."

Some of the horses and goats that come into the LARC have been neglected. They may have had little contact with people. They may be shy or wild. Workers do not train animals (such as horses) for riding, but they do work with the animals to get them used to a halter and lead rope. The animals are also taught to pick up their feet so the blacksmith can trim their hooves. The animals must learn how they are expected to behave from the people who work with them.

Communication is important. "You need to learn to communicate with animals so they will understand what you want them to do," Earlene says. "You also need to read their body language to know what they are feeling. Animals can tell you what kind of day they are having. They can sometimes tell you if something is wrong with them—but you need to learn to read their signals to understand." Some of the animals that Earlene sees have been hurt by people. "We teach them to trust humans again," she explains. "Animals are so forgiving. They don't hold grudges."

Safety around the animals is an important issue in this job. Anyone who works with large animals needs to be very careful. Some animals, like horses, llamas and cows, can move or kick unexpectedly. Everyone must stay on their toes. Workers need to be careful not only around the animals, but around the equipment too. They must make sure their clothes and fingers do not get caught on barbed-wire fences or in mowing or other equipment. Most of the work with large animals is often done outdoors. This means workers must also watch out for seasonal problems like wasps and heatstroke in summer and frostbite in winter. They must be prepared to do a lot of walking from one pasture or barn to another.

Working with large animals is physically demanding. People in this job are on their feet most of the day. The work requires strength and endurance. There are other difficult things about this job, though, such as seeing animals that are sick or that have been hurt by people.

Earlene feels good about her job, knowing that it benefits people and animals alike. "We give animals a second chance here. Some of them come to us in pretty bad shape. They may be unwanted, neglected or injured by their previous owners. We work with the animals to get them healthy and able to be around people again." The animals who are adopted bring pleasure to their new owners.

In addition to serving as a place where people can adopt animals, a large animal shelter like the LARC serves another important function. "It shows people that it takes a lot, both physically and financially, to take care of a large animal," says Earlene. "It helps people to know what they are getting into. We teach people who want to adopt an animal how to care for and communicate with that animal. This ensures that they will have a happier relationship with their new animal friend."

Could You Have a Career as a
Large Animal Shelter Director?

Does working with large animals sound good to you? Do you already have experience caring for a large animal such as a horse or cow? Maybe someday you can turn that experience into a career as a large animal shelter director. Here are some ideas you can explore right now:

1. Call your local humane society or animal control agency and find out what happens to unwanted or neglected large animals where you live. Is there a farm or large animal shelter where they can go to live?

2. If you have a large animal, do all you can to take good care of your pet. If you don't have a large animal of your own, perhaps you can find someone who does. Offer to help that person care for their pet.

3. Go to the library and read all you can about different kinds of large animals and how to care for them—not just horses, but also cows, burros, goats, sheep, pot-bellied pigs and llamas. Share what you learn with others.

chapter 7
ANIMAL SHELTER VETERINARIAN

Working at the ASPCA clinic in New York City gives Dr. Lila Miller a chance to help abandoned pets who have no other place to turn.

A-a-a-chew! The little puppy sneezed loudly. When he was first brought to the animal shelter, he was very sick. He was taken right to the clinic. There, the veterinary staff named him Liberty for the street where he had been found. Nursing Liberty back to health would be a big job. Pets that live on the streets risk many diseases, not to mention hunger and injury. Working with pets like Liberty is what makes Dr. Lila Miller's career so worthwhile.

Lila is an animal shelter veterinarian for the American Society for the Prevention of Cruelty to Animals (ASPCA) in New York City. She sees many sick and injured animals in her work. It is a challenge for a veterinarian to treat any sick or injured animal. It is even more challenging when the animal has been abandoned. "Seeing animals get a second chance is one of the biggest rewards of my job," says Lila.

The ASPCA is a large, national, nonprofit organization founded by Henry Bergh in 1866. In addition to its efforts to educate people about animals, the ASPCA runs an animal adoption center, an animal hospital, a national animal poison control center and the clinic where Lila works.

The main job of the animal shelter is to help animals find homes. Most animals are brought to the shelter because they are lost, because they have been abandoned or because their owners cannot keep them. The animal shelter veterinarian examines the animals to make sure they are healthy enough to be placed in a new home. If an animal is not healthy, the veterinarian treats the animal's illnesses or injuries.

The first thing that an animal shelter veterinarian does each day is conduct "rounds." This means examining all the animals and deciding what they need. "Animals can't tell you what is wrong," says Lila. "You have to figure out for yourself who is sick, who did not eat the night before, who needs additional shots or pills and who needs surgery." Lila has help with treating the animals. After she decides what the animals need, the veterinary technicians she works with take care of giving medicine and many of the treatments. This keeps Lila free to see new pets being brought into the clinic.

The animal shelter veterinarian helps to bring pets and people together. That's especially important in the city. There are lots of elderly people who don't have any family left. Pets help these people feel loved and important. An animal shelter clinic can sometimes help provide low-cost care so people on fixed incomes can keep their pets. There are children with emotional problems who, although they may not be able to talk to adults, may be able to bond with an animal. Having a pet from the shelter can make a big difference in the lives of these children. People with AIDS and other illnesses may be able to keep their pets longer through programs offered by the animal shelter. That's important, because everyone needs a friend when they are sick.

Lila wanted to be a veterinarian from the time she was six years old. Growing up in the city, she had a pet dog who came from the ASPCA. She was fascinated by animals and always knew she wanted to do something to help them. The path was not easy, however. Her high school guidance counselor actually tried to discourage Lila from following her dream. Lila did not let that stop her, though. She knew what she wanted to do.

Before you can work as a veterinarian at an animal shelter, you must complete many years of college veterinary training. When Lila entered college, she broke barriers. It was during a time when women were just beginning to gain acceptance as veterinarians. Previously, no more than one or two women at a time were allowed to enroll at her school. "People used to think women could not be veterinarians," says Lila. "They said women could not handle large animals. Or that women would drop out of school or leave their jobs to have children and not come back to work." Fighting all those stereotypes was difficult. But Lila did not give up. She was among the first women to graduate from the Cornell College of Veterinary Medicine, one of the finest veterinary medical schools in the United States.

Today things are different. Women now make up more than half the graduating class at Cornell. One thing that has not changed, though, is that being a veterinarian involves plenty of time, schooling and effort. Working hard at science and math is important. Graduating from high school with good grades in these subjects is a must. Then a prospective veterinarian's higher education begins. First is four years of college and an undergraduate degree—a bachelor of arts or bachelor of science. Next comes four years of veterinary medical school and a graduate degree—a doctorate. And after that are national and state licensing exams.

You might think being a veterinarian means you will spend all your time with animals. But being a veterinarian means spending a lot of time with people as well as animals. You have to give people advice about how to take care of their pets. And you have to do this in a way that shows you care about the people and their problems too. Patience is an important skill in veterinary work.

Why does an animal shelter veterinarian choose to work at a shelter and not in private practice? According to Lila, "When I got out of veterinary school, I knew there were lots of people working in private practice. I felt there were not enough people working to help homeless animals. I believed I could have more of an impact helping abandoned animals."

What advice does Lila have for anyone thinking about becoming an animal shelter veterinarian? "Remember that it takes eight years to become a veterinarian from the time you finish high school," Lila points out. "During that time, your friends and family will be advancing in their jobs, making more money. All the while, you will still be in school. When you get out, you won't make a huge salary working at an animal shelter. Animal shelter veterinary medicine is not a job to go into to get rich—at least not in terms of money," she says. As an animal shelter veterinarian, however, Dr. Lila Miller is rich in other ways—like knowing she is helping sick animals who have no place else to turn.

Could You Have a Career as an Animal Shelter Veterinarian?

Are you good at math and science? Are you ready to tackle eight years of college plus national and state licensing exams to reach your goal? How would you feel about making less money than most veterinarians who work in private practice? Here are some ideas to help you decide whether a career as an animal shelter veterinarian might be right for you:

1. Contact a veterinarian in your city or town and find out if you can volunteer to help out at a local animal hospital during afternoons or on weekends. Or try volunteering at your local animal shelter. Talk to staff members there who work in veterinary medicine.

2. Read all you can about being a veterinarian. One good book is *Animal Doctors* by Patricia Curtis. This book is out of print, but you may be able to locate it at your school or public library.

3. Talk with your teacher about doing an extra-credit math or science project with a veterinary theme.

chapter 8
DISASTER RELIEF SPECIALIST

The director of The HSUS Southeast Regional Office, Disaster Relief Specialist Laura Bevan, helps shelters and pet owners prepare and protect their pets in the event of a natural disaster.

© THE HUMANE SOCIETY OF THE UNITED STATES

Hurricanes, tornadoes, wildfires, floods! No matter where you live, you could be affected by some kind of natural disaster. It is one thing to hear about a disaster on the news. It is another when the police drive by your home announcing over a loudspeaker that you have to leave. What happens when there is a disaster? Many people just gather their belongings and head for the nearest emergency shelter. But there is a problem with this approach. Most public emergency shelters do not take pets. What do you do then?

Ask Laura Bevan. She works for The Humane Society of the United States (HSUS). She is the director of their Southeast Regional Office. She is also a humane disaster relief specialist. Laura does not work for a single animal shelter. Instead, when a hurricane or other disaster occurs, she assists the shelters that are affected.

What does a humane disaster relief specialist do? It depends on the disaster. For instance, when a disaster relief specialist learns that a hurricane is approaching, he or she begins by tracking the hurricane with the help of other disaster specialists. Together they track the storm's path by computer, television and radio. Once the disaster relief specialist knows which areas will likely be hit hardest, he or she calls the animal shelters in those areas. The shelter workers prepare animal crates and cages, collect pet food, buy bottled water and gather other supplies like flashlights and emergency generators.

Next the disaster relief specialist contacts people who are just outside the target areas of the hurricane—people who can help after the hurricane has passed. At the same time, the disaster relief specialist must prepare his or her own supplies, such as a sleeping bag, pillow, clothing, flashlight, food, drinking water, boots, life vest, cellular telephone and portable generator. If possible, the disaster relief specialist travels by car so he or she can bring additional needed equipment to the disaster areas.

The time comes for the disaster relief specialist to set out for the target areas with his or her team members. Sometimes the team may travel right behind the hurricane. All the while, they must stay in touch with other rescue teams by cellular telephone.

Imagine that you are part of Laura Bevan's humane disaster relief team and have just arrived at a disaster area. All around, you see houses with roofs missing. Fallen trees are everywhere, many of them lying across roads. Power lines are down. You cannot go near these power lines—it's too dangerous. You see a trailer house knocked over on its side, its door and windows smashed open. You see a truck lying upside down, tossed by powerful winds. Suddenly, from under the truck, you hear a muffled whine—a dog has found safety there from the wind and rain. You rescue your first animal victim.

"When you arrive at a disaster area," says Laura, "there's a lot to do. First, you need to get a 'go-ahead' from emergency officials. Once you have their permission to get started, the main job on Day One is to see how bad things are. Of course, you rescue any animals you find. But at this point, you don't go looking for them." To prepare, Laura may need to set up a temporary shelter or locate boats to use in rescuing animals. She also tells the local media that people should look for lost pets at the animal shelter or temporary shelter.

"By Day Two," Laura explains, "you are ready to start rescue operations. If there is flooding, as there often is after a hurricane, animals caught in the flood need to be rescued first. We go out in boats and rescue animals from just about every place you can imagine," she says. "There may be animals stranded on rooftops or in trees. Some animals may have found shelter on the second floor of their homes or other people's homes. All of them have to be gotten out safely."

The team also looks for animals that are running loose, trapped in houses or caught in the rubble that once was a house. The temporary shelter is full of activity too. The workers set up crates and cages for the dogs and cats. As the pets wait for their owners, they receive food as well as an examination by a veterinarian. The rescue operations may continue into Day Three. "We also put out food for the animals we can't catch," Laura explains.

"By Day Four," she says, "we may start using box traps to catch the animals that are still out there living in the rubble of their old homes. The box traps will not hurt them." Once caught, the animals are taken to the animal shelter or temporary shelter to wait for their owners.

Sometimes people ask Laura why she is helping animal victims instead of human victims. "By the time we come onto the scene, most of the people have left the area or been rescued," says Laura. "The animals, however, are still out there. Some of them are injured. All of them are afraid. Pain and fear are the same whether they are experienced by a person or an animal. Our job is to relieve suffering wherever we find it."

After the emergency is over, there is still plenty of work to do. The disaster relief specialist continues to help animals by teaching pet owners how to protect their pets in an emergency. The single most important thing owners can do is to take their pets with them if they have to leave home. It is also important to make sure pets wear ID tags and that a cage, box or crate is kept handy for emergency travel.

In her role as a disaster relief specialist, Laura teaches people about preparing for emergencies in many ways. She writes articles, does television interviews and answers questions over the telephone. She gives speeches about the need to prepare for pets in the event of a disaster. She is a rescue worker, manager, teacher and writer as well as a public speaker. Her skill at performing all these jobs helps make Laura a successful humane disaster relief specialist.

Could You Have a Career as a Humane Disaster Relief Specialist?

Are you the kind of person who stays calm in a crisis? Are you comfortable directing others? Do you like writing, and speaking in front of a group? If so, a career as a humane disaster relief specialist might be right for you. Here are some ideas to help you decide for yourself:

1. Notice how you react when faced with a challenge or difficulty. Are you calm and collected? Are you good at thinking on your feet? Make a list of reasons why you think you would be good at helping out in an emergency.

2. Practice teaching others how to protect their pets in a disaster. Start with your family. Talk to your parents about taking pets with you in an emergency, having a pet carrier handy at all times, and making sure your pet wears license and ID tags.

3. Learn all you can about disaster relief from your local Red Cross. Find out if they are affiliated with an animal shelter that will keep pets safe if their owners should need to stay in an emergency shelter.

4. Ask The Humane Society of the United States for information on preparing for disasters. Write to: Disaster Services, HSUS, 2100 L Street, NW, Washington, D.C. 20037.

part two
Careers in Veterinary Medicine

Entertainer Will Rogers once commented, "The best doctor in the world is the veterinarian. His patients can't tell him what is wrong. He just has to know."

Disease and injury can be like a puzzle. There are clues to the puzzle, but the answer is not always easy to find, even for humans. Still, a human patient can tell you what hurts. An animal cannot. A veterinarian needs to learn to read the signs that tell what is wrong.

The Work of the Veterinarian

When people think of careers that help animals, the job of the veterinarian is often what comes to mind first. You may have considered becoming a veterinarian yourself because you want to care for animals and keep them free from pain.

The veterinarian's job is to keep animals healthy. In the case of a sick or injured animal, the veterinarian must figure out what kind of disease or injury the animal has. He or she must prescribe or suggest treatment, and may need to perform surgery.

There are many different kinds of veterinarians. Those of us who have pets are familiar with the work of the small animal veterinarian. This animal doctor generally treats dogs, cats, and small mammal pets such as guinea pigs, rabbits, ferrets, rats and hamsters. We take our pets to the small animal veterinarian for yearly checkups and vaccinations, for spaying or neutering operations and for medical care when they are sick.

Some veterinarians, however, choose to specialize or focus on just one kind of animal medicine. A veterinary dermatologist, for example, only treats animals who have skin diseases. Other veterinarians focus on treating a particular kind of animal. Some treat only cats. Others treat only large animals, like horses and cows. Still others treat only wild animals.

A Veterinarian's Education

Whatever area of medicine a veterinarian pursues, many years of training are required. Just to apply for enrollment at a veterinary medical college, you need an undergraduate degree and a number of pre-veterinary courses. Which courses you need depends on the school you want to attend.

Once accepted into a college of veterinary medicine, a student begins his or her studies by taking classes that have a strong emphasis on math and science. Typical subjects include chemistry, physiology, anatomy and biology. Later, a veterinary student is expected to complete some lab work. In time, the studies become more hands-on as the student focuses on clinical and surgical training.

After four years and many hours of study and training, the veterinary student graduates. Yet he or she must still pass exams to become certified—that is, meet state licensing requirements—before going into practice. And to remain certified, a veterinarian must typically take courses in later years to keep up his or her skills. Some veterinarians also take additional training to practice a special area of animal medicine—marine mammal veterinary studies, for instance. State and federal permits are also required for those who wish to practice wildlife veterinary medicine. Even after obtaining all the permits and licenses, a veterinarian must keep up with each new treatment and breakthrough in animal medicine.

Veterinary Careers

There are many different kinds of jobs open to veterinarians. Most veterinary school graduates work as small animal veterinarians in private practice. About 75 percent of the veterinarians in the United States fall into this category.

Some veterinarians work at animal shelters. They treat homeless pets who are sick or injured. Other veterinarians work full-time for wildlife rehabilitation centers. Their patients are native wild animals such as squirrels, chipmunks, raccoons, geese, ducks and turtles. Still other veterinarians do not work in these typical hospital settings. They may teach or work for a large, nonprofit organization like The Humane Society of the United States.

Working with Others

No matter what kind of work a veterinarian does to help animals, he or she must care about people as well. In the case of pets and farm animals, each patient usually has an owner. If the animal is sick or injured, the owner may be worried or distressed. In the case of wild animals brought to a rehabilitation center, almost all are brought in by a person who has concerns about the animal's welfare. Learning to deal with the emotions of concerned humans is as much a part of the job as treating the animals is.

Most veterinarians must be team players. They don't do all the work of treating animals themselves. They usually work side by side with veterinary technicians and other assistants. Veterinarians rely on their assistants to care as much about animals and people as they do.

The Veterinary Technician

In today's modern animal hospitals, a wide variety of medical tasks are performed. Just like hospitals for humans, animal hospitals have different rooms for surgery, special treatments and examinations. And just like medical procedures performed on humans, many of the veterinary procedures performed on animals require sophisticated equipment. To help veterinarians, many animal hospitals employ assistants who have some medical training and technical expertise.

One person who assists a veterinarian is the veterinary technician. This person performs a variety of medical duties. Performing routine tests on blood, urine and stool, assisting the veterinarian during surgery, keeping track of an animal's progress and giving treatments that the veterinarian has prescribed are all part of the veterinary technician's job. Because the veterinary technician interacts with many people, he or she must be able to work well with others.

To prepare for their work, some veterinary technicians attend a two-year college that offers an animal technical program. Others attend a four-year college that offers a bachelor of science degree in veterinary technology. Courses often include biology, chemistry, anatomy, communications and mathematics. Many schools expect students to spend their summers getting practical job-related experience at an animal hospital.

Like the veterinarian, the veterinary technician also must be licensed by the state in which he or she wishes to work. This means the individual must take special tests after college to become registered to work as a veterinary technician.

The Veterinary Assistant

The job of the veterinary technician should not be confused with that of the veterinary assistant. A veterinary assistant focuses mostly on kennel care and restraining animals, rather than on formal medical duties. Depending on the animal hospital, the veterinary assistant may also admit pets into the hospital and help with keeping some of the records.

Veterinary assistants are not expected to complete the same kind of medical training required of veterinary technicians. A high school diploma is usually required, and classes in subjects like biology and chemistry may be helpful.

Choosing Your Career

Whether you want a career as a veterinarian or a veterinary technician, there are many different kinds of work to be done. The following chapters will give you ideas about some of these areas of veterinary medicine. Also, be sure to see Chapter 7, which explores the career of an animal shelter veterinarian, and Chapter 18, which explores the career of a specialized veterinary technician who works with marine mammals.

chapter 9
SMALL ANIMAL VETERINARIAN

Dr. Thomas Arand examines a patient at his animal hospital in Round Rock, Texas.

© DR. THOMAS ARAND

A man in a white doctor's coat stands at the front of a classroom full of students. "Okay … one last time!" urges the man. "What do you do when a strange dog comes up to you on the playground?" A chorus of young voices shouts the answer, "Stand like a tree!"

"You've got it!" declares Dr. Thomas Arand, a small animal veterinarian in Round Rock, Texas. He has just finished speaking to a group of elementary students about how to avoid being bitten by a dog. In addition to his work healing pets, Tom likes to teach this important pet-related safety lesson to students. But more about that later.

Tom describes the animal hospital where he works as "a typical small animal practice." He works there with one other veterinarian, several veterinary technicians and a clerical staff. The animal hospital is somewhat like a hospital for humans. There are exam rooms, a reception area and a surgery room.

Like Tom, most veterinarians start each day by treating their animal patients that are already in the hospital. Most of the animals have had surgery or other treatments the day before. The veterinarian checks their condition. He or she may take blood, urine, stool or other samples. Blood samples, in particular, can tell the veterinarian a lot about whether an animal is healthy. The veterinarian or the veterinary technician may also give medicine and any shots that are needed.

Next, the veterinarian sees the animals that are being brought in for examinations that day. He or she looks carefully at each animal, weighs the animal and listens to the animal's heart with a stethoscope. In fact, the exam is a lot like the exam a human patient might receive. The veterinarian may also take blood or other samples at this point, and give medicine or shots. He or she listens closely to the pet owner's concerns and tries to learn what is wrong with the animal.

Sometimes the difficulty is not a problem with the animal's physical health. It is a problem with how owner and pet interact. "A big part of my job is teaching owners how to take care of their pets properly," says Tom. "Often, when a pet is having a problem, it is not the animal's fault, but the owner's." For instance, a cat who scratches furniture may not have been given a scratching post or may not have been trained to use one. A dog who barks may just be lonely and trying to get his owner to spend more time with him. Tom advises pet owners about how to live with and care for their pets so problems like these can be managed.

The veterinarian also performs surgery. At many animal hospitals, surgery is scheduled during specific times. The animals are anesthetized first—that is, they are given medicine to make them sleep so they will not feel any pain during the operation. Throughout the surgery, the veterinarian and his or her assistants watch the level of anesthesia very carefully. In Tom's practice, he does "many different kinds of surgery, from spay and neuter operations to fixing broken limbs, to dealing with some kinds of cancer." As the animals recover from surgery, the veterinarian continues to check their progress. If they are sore or in pain, the veterinarian gives them a padded cage and/or pain medication. Throughout the surgery process, the veterinary technicians and assistants help care for the animals too.

Tom enjoys his work because it helps both people and animals. As an animal doctor, he finds it satisfying to make sick animals well. But there is more to his job. "My work also benefits people," he says. "The human-animal bond is very important." Studies show that having a pet actually helps people live longer—by lowering their blood pressure, for instance. "If I can help make a better relationship between a person and their pet," says Tom, "then it benefits the owner as well as the animal. Also, when pets suffer, their owners suffer. That is why it is so important to me to do everything possible to ensure that people's pets get the very best care there is."

In his spare time, Tom teaches children about pets. As a veterinarian, he has heard many stories about children who have been bitten by dogs. So he developed his own program to teach young people how to avoid a dog bite.

"I felt it was something that kids really needed," says Tom. "Several children in our area were seriously bitten by dogs. You see, kids are just the right height to get bitten badly. The problem," he says, "is that dogs are excited by the chase. If you stand still, a strange dog will probably leave you alone. But if you run, he will chase you just for the excitement of it." That can be a problem—because a child cannot outrun a dog.

"Here's what I teach kids," says Tom. "Rule Number One is 'Never pet a strange dog.' If you don't know the animal, stay away. Rule Number Two is 'Don't go near a strange dog.' But if one comes up to you, don't run off yelling. That will only excite the dog and may result in a bite. Instead, you have to stay very still and quiet. I teach kids to 'Stand like a tree' or 'Lie like a log.'" Tom actually has his students practice this technique. Putting it into practice helps children remember what to do the next time a strange dog approaches them.

Working to heal animals and helping children stay safe around pets are both enjoyable parts of Tom's career. What else does he like about his work? That's easy: "The animals themselves," says Tom. "Every veterinarian loves the challenge of saving an animal," he explains. "You like to be able to say, 'This animal was sick and I made him well again.' But what I really enjoy most is the reaction I get from that animal that is just overjoyed to see me when I get to work in the morning. If you think about it, most people don't have that where they work—someone who is really glad to see them. The puppy that greets you with a ton of kisses somehow makes it all worthwhile."

Being a veterinarian involves years of education and lots of hard work. Still, most small animal veterinarians would agree that many rewards come with working in this demanding career.

Could You Have a Career as a Small Animal Veterinarian?

Years of education, lots of hard work, patience and dedication—these are some of the things you'll need to become a small animal veterinarian. Here are some other things to consider if you think this career might be right for you:

1. Are you good at math and science? Improve your skills even more. Ask your teacher if you can do a special math or science project related to animals.

2. Do you love a mystery? Figuring out what is wrong with an animal is a little like being a detective. Interview a local veterinarian. Find out what kinds of "medical mysteries" he or she has unraveled. Share what you learn with your classmates.

3. If possible, volunteer to help out at your local animal hospital during afternoons or on weekends. You'll learn a lot about animals—and about yourself.

chapter 10
WILDLIFE VETERINARIAN

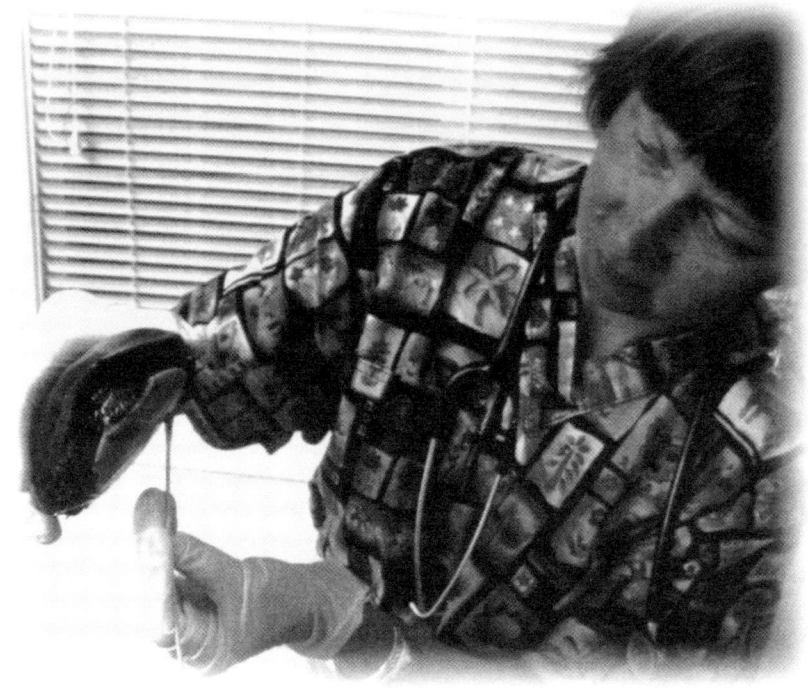

Dr. Patrice Klein helps turtles, skunks, squirrels, songbirds, and many other kinds of wildlife at The HSUS Wildlife Rehabilitation Training Center.

The large, female snapping turtle glided through the pale green pond. She had spent the past fifty years here. She was not even aware that she was sharing the pond with people who liked to fish.

Suddenly the sunlight caught a bright, shiny object. It danced before the turtle's eyes like a tasty minnow. She snapped at it quickly. But it was not a minnow. Someone's fishing line had become tangled and the hook and line had been cut and left to drift in the water. Now the snapping turtle had a fishing hook stuck fast inside her throat, and a tangled line hanging out of her mouth.

Fortunately the turtle came out of the water and was found by a woman who lived nearby. She called her local animal control agency. The animal control officer came to the pond, coaxed and prodded the enormous, twenty-five-pound turtle into a sturdy box and took her to The Humane Society of the United States Wildlife Rehabilitation Training Center (HSUS-WRTC) in West Barnstable, Massachusetts. There the turtle was cared for by Dr. Patrice Klein, a wildlife veterinarian.

At this unique training center and wild animal hospital, Pat examined the turtle. "Snapping turtles can be very dangerous if you don't know how to handle them properly," she says. "They can spin around to face you with amazing speed. Then as you move right, they move right; as you move left, they move left. I call it 'the turtle dance,'" she laughs.

Pat began by pulling gently on the fishing line to see if it could be removed easily, but the hook was stuck fast. X-rays showed Pat exactly where it was located. She decided to take the hook out surgically. First the turtle was given medication to help her relax. Then a tube was put into her windpipe (the airway leading to her lungs) and she was given a special gas to make her sleep while the surgery was performed.

"Turtles [which are reptiles] take longer to heal than mammals," says Pat. "It took a couple of weeks for her to recover. After that, we contacted the animal control officer, who took the turtle back to her pond and released her. It is especially important for wild animals to be returned to the area they came from. They know how to find food there and stay safe."

The HSUS Wildlife Rehabilitation Training Center is a busy place. Five to ten student interns work there at any given time. While one person handles wildlife calls (up to sixty per day), another may be working in the kitchen to prepare lots of little animal meals. Yet another is examining animals in the wards. Meanwhile, someone else is busy cleaning cages. Baby animals can make a terrible mess overnight! Another intern might be working in the laboratory doing x-rays or testing blood samples. More animals arrive each day, so workers must be prepared to handle whatever wild animal emergencies come through the door.

In addition to the animal wards inside the hospital, there are pens and cages outside for recovering animals. Raccoons, skunks, squirrels, songbirds, hawks and gulls all may be mending at any given time. There are large flight cages for songbirds and a five-hundred-gallon swimming pool for recovering ducks and geese. The goal is to get the animals healthy and back to their homes in the wild with as little human contact as possible. This highly developed facility is an ideal workplace for a wildlife veterinarian.

Like any animal doctor, the wildlife veterinarian must complete veterinary medical school and pass licensing exams. He or she must be a detail-oriented individual with a lot of patience and a strong love of animals. But wildlife veterinary work does not always take place in a hospital setting like The HSUS Wildlife Rehabilitation Training Center. Sometimes you have to go where the animals are. For instance, you might work with the U.S. Fish and Wildlife Service to build up the population of bighorn sheep or endangered whooping cranes. In that case, you would need to be in good physical condition, would need to know how to protect yourself when working in the field, and would need to be comfortable working in all kinds of weather.

The successful wildlife veterinarian understands that wild animals are very different from pets. "Wild animals are not comforted the way you comfort a frightened dog or cat," explains Pat. "A wild animal does not want to be held or petted. Also, the goal of treating a wild animal is not to keep the animal in captivity. Wild animals belong in the wild."

As the wildlife veterinarian for The Humane Society of the United States, Pat performs a variety of duties. In addition to her work at the training center, she is involved in field projects. In one field project, Pat helped test a new form of birth control for white-tailed deer and wild horses. In some parts of the country, these animals have no natural predators. That might not be a problem if people did not want to use the land where these animals live. But as the human population increases, the available space animals decreases. So sometimes a decision is made to limit the size of certain animal populations. Pat helped to prove that an injected form of birth control is safe for wildlife and that it works in keeping a deer herd, for instance, at a certain population size.

Pat also teaches classes for wildlife rehabilitators. She has helped design workshops for animal control officers and others who work with wildlife. She is also involved in legislative work. When a proposed law that would help protect wildlife is being debated at the state legislature, Pat may go to the hearing to testify on behalf of the animals. With her expertise, lawmakers listen.

Many wildlife veterinarians do not have as varied a job as Pat does. However, they do work daily with wild animals in hospital and/or field settings. They strive continuously to keep up with the latest discoveries in the care and treatment of wild animals. Like Pat, they share a strong appreciation for and commitment to wild animals and their habitats.

© THE HUMANE SOCIETY OF THE UNITED STATES

This snapping turtle was released back to her home in the wild after her broken shell was patched up and healed at The HSUS Wildlife Rehabilitation Training Center.

Could You Have a Career as a Wildlife Veterinarian?

A person who is interested in becoming a wildlife veterinarian should be good at math and science. You should also be prepared to attend college for many years and to work long hours. But if you love wild animals, a career as a wildlife veterinarian might be right for you. In the meantime, explore these ideas:

1. Find out which veterinarians in your area treat wild animals. You can do this by calling your local animal control agency or humane society—or by calling the veterinarians themselves. Make a list of these telephone numbers and post it with other important emergency numbers. Then talk to a wildlife veterinarian. Find out if you can volunteer to help out at an animal hospital, wildlife rehabilitation center or nature center.

2. Tell your friends what to do if they ever find an injured wild animal. Share these rules: (1) Never touch the animal yourself, (2) always find an adult to help and (3) contact a veterinarian. Some veterinarians will treat wild animals free of charge. If your local veterinarian has questions about treating a wild animal, ask him or her to call The HSUS Wildlife Rehabilitation Training Center, (508) 362-0111.

3. If you are interested in being a wildlife veterinarian, it is never too early to start learning about wild animals—where they live, what they eat and what their needs are. Read all you can about wild animals, especially the animals native to your part of the country.

chapter 11
LARGE ANIMAL VETERINARIAN

Dr. Paul Michelsen checks the teeth of his patient, Kola the horse.

A newborn foal lay in a wet heap on the grass. The mother horse gently pushed her tiny baby with her nose. He was only a few hours old. But foals like little Norman usually stand within a few hours of being born. Something was wrong.

"Norman did not receive enough oxygen during birth," says his veterinarian, Dr. Paul Michelsen. "He needed lots of care. It meant staying up all night many nights in a row, giving him medicine and fluids." Thanks to his veterinarian's special care, Norman finally grew from a baby that could not stand into a healthy adult horse.

Dr. Paul Michelsen is a large animal veterinarian in Potter Valley, California. Just how large is large? Large is when your patient eats fourteen pounds of food a day, drinks ten gallons of water and weighs one thousand pounds. Often, many of a large animal veterinarian's patients are horses—and they fit that description perfectly.

Like most large animal veterinarians, Paul treats mainly horses, cows, sheep and goats. He also treats some pot-bellied pigs and llamas. One of the main differences between working with large animals and working with small ones is the travel time involved. "Generally," says Paul, "my patients don't come to me. I go to them."

A typical day for the large animal veterinarian begins with a series of appointments and visits. For instance, the veterinarian might be called on to perform surgery on a horse. The veterinarian and an assistant drive to the location in a truck packed carefully with equipment. Everything they need must be at hand. "Recently," explains Paul, "I had to perform surgery on a horse that had a bone chip in his leg. I kept the horse under anesthesia while my partner did the surgery."

Imagine performing surgery right out in the sunlight on the front lawn! "That is how horse surgery is sometimes done in a farm practice," says Paul. "A lawn is actually a pretty sterile place." Before any surgery can be done, the veterinarian must make routine preparations. In the area of the animal's body where the surgery is to be performed, the animals' hair is clipped and its skin is scrubbed. Then the veterinarian gives the animal anesthesia or other pain-control medication.

As the anesthesia begins to take effect, there are plenty of things to be thinking about—like not getting in the way of a horse who is about to lie down. At the same time, the veterinarian has to help the animal lie down so that the area the veterinarian will be working on is facing up. As the surgery begins, the veterinarian must monitor the animal's breathing and control the amount of anesthesia—too much can hurt the animal, and too little can cause the animal to feel pain from the surgery.

In addition to surgery, there are other routine procedures to be done on large animals. "In our practice, we do a lot of vaccinations and de-worming," explains Paul. "If a horse has eaten too much grain, I might have to pump the animal's stomach. This involves putting a tube into the horse's nose, down his throat and into his stomach to get the grain out. Then we treat his stomach with antacids, laxatives and other medicine." Treating large animals is rewarding work, but it can also be dirty, smelly and difficult.

Understanding both the physical and the emotional needs of animals helps the large animal veterinarian in his or her work. "Much of what I do to animals is painful or at least uncomfortable," says Paul. "So I try to make friends with an animal, such as a horse, before doing something like giving him a shot or working on his teeth. For example, I might approach a horse by lowering my head and blowing into his nostrils. That is how horses greet each other. This may look funny to someone watching, but it says to the animal that I am not a threat. By understanding an animal's behavior, I find I can communicate better with that animal." When an animal—especially a large animal—is calm and doesn't feel threatened, the veterinarian's job is much easier.

Paul's influence goes beyond the animals he treats in his practice. "I used my knowledge of animals' physical and emotional needs to help develop standards of care for raising farm animals. It is my hope that people who raise animals on farms will learn from these standards. When animals are treated humanely, it is not only better for the animals. It's better for the farm as a business as well," he says.

The things that Paul likes best about what he does are "working with animals and the people who own them and doing something different every day." He sometimes finds the long hours tiring and difficult. There are plenty of emergency calls in the middle of night. "It is part of what I do," says Paul, "but it can be tough on me and my family."

Being a large animal veterinarian means working closely with people as well as animals. "Some people," says Paul, "are drawn to veterinary medicine because they are more comfortable with animals than they are with humans. Often these people are not very successful veterinarians. That's because every animal has a person attached to him or her. You can't focus on just the animal, because more often than not, an animal's problems have to do with how that animal is being cared for by an owner. I am as much a psychiatrist as an animal doctor," laughs Paul. "In addition to treating the animal, I treat the person and his or her relationship with that animal."

What advice does Paul have for young people interested in a career as a large animal veterinarian? "Veterinary work is very satisfying. But don't romanticize what the actual work involves," he warns. Paul teaches an afterschool class for youth in his town. "I purposely make the class as unglamorous as possible," he says. "In one of the first sessions, I have everyone bring in a fecal sample from their pets. Then they examine it for parasites and eggs. I try to let my students know that being a veterinarian is not all puppies and kittens. There is a lot of dirt and heartache that goes along with the job." Dirt, heartache and helping animals are what being a large animal veterinarian is all about.

© STEPHANIE ROMM

"Helping animal patients like this ewe and her lamb is very satisfying work, but it is not always easy," says Dr. Paul Michelsen.

Could You Have a Career as a Large Animal Veterinarian?

It takes patience to attend college for many years and to work long hours. But if you love working around horses and other large animals, a career as a large animal veterinarian might be one of the most rewarding you could have. Explore these ideas and decide for yourself:

1. Many large animal veterinarians work in rural areas. Would you like to live in such an area? Are you physically strong? Do you think you would be able to work with animals who are big and sometimes aggressive? Make a list of reasons why you think you would be good at this type of work. Share your list with a friend or family member.

2. Write to the American Veterinary Medical Association, 1931 N. Meacham Rd., Suite 100, Schaumburg, IL 60173-4360, and ask for information about the work of the large animal veterinarian. Or check out their website at http://www.avma.org/. Most of the information that this organization offers is for adults, but you and your parents may enjoy sharing it together.

3. Read all you can about the work of the large animal veterinarian. James Herriot was a British veterinarian who treated many different kinds of animals both large and small. His stories have inspired animal lovers all around the world. His books are written for adults, but you and your parents will be sure to enjoy sharing them together. Check your library for these titles: *All Creatures Great and Small, All Things Bright and Beautiful, All Things Wise and Wonderful* and *The Lord God Made Them All.*

chapter 12
VETERINARY TECHNICIAN

Ron Sampson's job as a veterinary technician is full of surprises.

The black-and-white mutt was a sorry sight when he arrived at the clinic. He had licked at a pool of antifreeze on the floor of his owner's garage and was very sick. Antifreeze tastes sweet to animals. Yet antifreeze that contains a certain chemical (ethylene glycol) is poisonous. In an emergency like this, you have to act fast. Fortunately, Ron Sampson, a veterinary technician at Jane's Vet Clinic in Washington, D.C., knew just what to do. He began to give the dog charcoal to coat his stomach and keep the poison from harming him. "With animals who have eaten something dangerous, we often give charcoal," says Ron. "It is in the form of a black liquid—sort of like maple syrup."

One thing Ron likes about his job is that it is full of surprises. As Ron explains, "I was using a tube to try to get the charcoal down the dog's throat. Even though the dog was very sick, it was a real struggle. He was not having any of it. After many tries, I finally gave up. I let my patient get down off the examination table." With that, the dog walked over to where a bowl of the black liquid had been set down on the floor. He began drinking the charcoal on his own. He did very well afterward and recovered. "Animals are full of surprises," says Ron. This is part of what makes his work as a veterinary technician so interesting.

The veterinarian's job would be much more difficult if it were not for the veterinary technician. A veterinary technician does not pursue the same long, demanding studies as an animal doctor. Yet the work he or she performs is no less important to the health and well-being of animals. Being a successful veterinary technician takes just as much hard work, cooperation and patience as any job in animal medicine.

Veterinary technicians are found in many different work settings. They may work at animal hospitals, animal shelters or wildlife rescue centers. Some veterinary technicians take special courses or pursue special experience to qualify for work with certain kinds of animals—large animals or marine mammals, for instance. The majority of veterinary technicians, however, work in animal hospitals, where they perform a wide variety of important tasks. This is part of what keeps the job lively. Most of the veterinary technician's work involves direct contact with animals and people.

Like a veterinarian, the veterinary technician begins each morning by checking all the animals who spent the night in the clinic. Each animal has a medical chart, which helps both the veterinarian and the veterinary technician keep track of the animal's treatments. The regular duties of the veterinary technician include anything and everything that assists the veterinarian, from cleaning an animal's teeth to giving shots and pills. The veterinary technician also helps with first aid—such as cleaning and bandaging wounds—and takes blood, urine, stool and other samples.

Before the veterinarian examines an animal, the veterinary technician may check the animal's heart rate and weight, and record the information. Like a veterinarian, the veterinary technician must be good at science and at keeping track of details. Information must be written down carefully. A mistake can be costly—and could even result in harm to the animal.

In the operating room, the veterinary technician often assists the veterinarian as surgery is performed on an animal. For instance, Ron sometimes helps with administering anesthesia—the medication used to keep an animal from feeling pain during surgery. Or he may keep watch over an animal during an operation. He makes sure that the animal's heart rate, breathing and body temperature remain normal.

Some veterinary technicians help with other tasks too—like the day-to-day management of an animal hospital. This means working with the public and talking to pet owners. If a pet owner is worried about his or her animal's health, the situation can be stressful. The veterinary technician must also do a lot of physical work. This might involve moving animals from one room to another. It might mean holding animals while the veterinarian examines and treats them.

The veterinary technician at a small animal clinic must be comfortable working with all kinds of animals. Cats, however, are the pet of choice among the pet owners who visit the clinic where Ron works. "Many of the people who bring their pets here have office jobs," he explains. "Keeping a cat works well with their schedules." Ron enjoys working with cats as well as with dogs and other animals.

Education is also part of the veterinary technician's job. Sometimes people need to learn how to train their pets, so that pet owner and pet can live together happily. "I try to help people understand why their pet is doing one thing or another," says Ron. "It's surprising, but many pet owners just don't understand the basics of animal behavior. Client education is the biggest thing I feel I can do to help both animals and people. I try to help people get to know their pets better, to have a better relationship with them."

The veterinary technician must care a great deal about animals and people. It takes strength and patience to work with animals—many of whom don't understand that you are trying to help them. It takes good communication skills to help a pet owner correct an animal's bad habits rather than give up on keeping the pet altogether. It takes compassion to comfort pets who are afraid or in pain. "There is nothing better, however," says Ron, "than seeing a sick animal recover and knowing you helped to make that happen."

Could You Have a Career as a **Veterinary Technician?**

Maybe you're saying to yourself, "I'm pretty good at math and science—and I love working with animals. But I'm not sure I want to spend all those years in school before I can begin working." You might want to consider becoming a veterinary technician. Here are some ideas to help you decide for yourself:

1. Think about a time when you had to take responsibility for an animal. What did you do? Were you good at making decisions in the animal's best interest? Next, make a list of all the qualities you have that would help you be a successful veterinary technician. Finally, make a list of reasons why this career might not be right for you.

2. Find out more about the work of the veterinary technician by writing to the North American Veterinary Technician Association, P.O. Box 224, Battle Ground, IN 47920, or by visiting their website at http://www.avma.org/navta/. This organization offers information for adults, but you and your parents may enjoy sharing it together.

3. If possible, volunteer to help out at a local animal hospital or animal shelter during afternoons or on weekends. You'll learn a lot about animals—and about yourself. Also, take the opportunity to talk to a veterinary technician who works there. Ask that person to tell you about his or her career.

part three
Careers Working with Pets

In today's busy world, pet owners sometimes need a little help. They may need someone to assist with training their pet—teaching their dog to "sit," "stay" and "heel," for instance. They may need someone to groom their pet—to help keep their animal tidy and flea-free. Or they may need assistance getting their pet from one place to another. Pet owners may also need someone to care for their pet while they are away. A wide range of businesses provide supplies and services to assist pet owners and help maintain healthy pets.

Providing a Service to People and Pets

Dog trainers, dog groomers, kennel managers, pet-sitters and pet taxi drivers all provide a service to pet owners. Some service jobs may be connected with the work of an animal shelter. More often, though, they are the result of an enterprising person who cares deeply about animals and wants a job that involves direct contact with our furred and feathered friends.

Many people who start a career providing a service to pet owners begin by working for someone else. Often, the training for such work is on-the-job, although there are a few schools that offer formal training in such areas as dog grooming and kennel management. In the case of pet-sitters, professional certification is not required, but is available.

Job Qualifications

To be successful, an individual who wants to work with pets must be good at relating to animals. Often this means understanding an animal's natural behavior. Learning more about animal behavior can be as simple as making daily observations of how your own pet or a friend's pet behaves (this can teach you a lot about animals—and can even be a terrific humane science project).

A general understanding of pet health is also important for people who want to work with pets. This is especially true if the person will be responsible for an animal's care in the absence of the owner. This knowledge can come from simply owning the same kind of pet that you will be taking care of for others. It can also come from volunteering at an animal shelter or veterinary hospital.

Physical strength is sometimes required in providing animal care services. A pet usually won't get into a pet taxi without help from the driver. Patience is often needed as well—such as when a pet hides under the sofa the moment the pet-sitter comes to feed and water the animal in the owner's absence.

Providing services to pet owners often involves more than just caring for animals. If the service provider is self-employed, he or she must have good business, organizational and management skills. Customers must be billed and payments must be kept track of. There may be a need for doing other kinds of paperwork as well. For instance, written permission or instructions from owners regarding special care for their pets may need to be obtained and organized. Advertising is necessary to inform people about available services. A workplace may need to be established and properly maintained for customers and visitors.

Working as an Obedience Trainer

Some people just have a natural ability to communicate with animals. Maybe you are one of them. The greatest number of obedience trainers work with dogs. Trainers are often called upon to teach dogs the basics of proper canine behavior around humans.

Walking on a leash without pulling, following basic commands like "sit" and "stay" and not jumping on guests are all good rules for dogs. And puppies must be housetrained.

Some people gain their expertise in obedience training by attending school; others, by working as an apprentice to an established dog trainer. And still others learn through their work in law enforcement or the military. There are currently no official standards for training facilities, so anyone who is thinking of attending a dog training academy needs to do some homework. Before you apply as a student to any obedience training school, it is important to speak to recent graduates—be sure that their experience is one you want to repeat. In the meantime, the National Association of Dog Obedience Instructors and other organizations are working toward setting professional standards for certifying licensed dog trainers. If you are considering dog training as a career, you will want to be part of this growing trend toward professionalism and high standards in the obedience training field.

Pet-Sitting as a Profession

Some people who love animals and know how to care for them make a career out of caring for other people's pets. In our mobile society, many individuals need to be away from home for work as well as vacations. The saying goes that a change is good for you—if you're a human, that is. Dogs and cats are not usually interested in changing their surroundings just for fun. Most pets are happier remaining in the home environment. For people who must travel, the pet-sitter provides care for the pet and peace of mind for the owner.

Working as a pet-sitter involves keeping detailed records of each pet and the animal's needs. A pet-sitter goes into other people's homes, so he or she must be reliable and trustworthy. It is not enough to care for a pet if you leave without remembering to lock the door behind you. Many pet-sitters are bonded and insured. This helps protect them in case an owner later accuses the pet-sitter of negligence in caring for the pet or in caring for the owner's home.

Some people come to their work as pet-sitters by caring for the pets of their friends and neighbors and gradually building a business through word of mouth. Others start out by assisting a pet-sitter who is currently in business. As with obedience training, there are currently no official standards for pet-sitting. However, as more and more pet-related businesses are established, professional standards and certification may become part of the pet-sitting profession.

Getting Pets from One Place to Another

Want to ride the bus with your cat? Sorry, but pets—other than Seeing Eye and Hearing Ear dogs—are not allowed on public transportation. What's an owner without a car to do? The answer can be found in the pet transportation business. It is a small but growing field—especially in today's cities, where many people rely on public transit and therefore do not have cars.

The pet taxi driver does not need formal education or training. However, he or she does need to be an entrepreneur—that is, someone who can run and maintain their own company, keep records, manage billing, advertise the business and so on. A pet taxi driver needs an insured car or van, pet carriers, a good knowledge of the streets in his or her area and some form of personal insurance. He or she must be reliable, courteous to pet owners and knowledgeable about pets and their needs.

Choosing Your Career

The best way to learn about a career that involves working with pets is often to talk to someone in that profession. Volunteering in a related area can also be helpful. As with other career paths, it is important to get as much information as you can. Then decide for yourself.

Providing a service for pet owners can be a rewarding experience. It takes good judgment, hard work and a genuine concern for animals. Although the pay is often low when starting out, a person in such a job can often look forward to being his or her own boss eventually, if not from the very start. This can lead to another source of job satisfaction—knowing that your success or failure is due entirely to your own efforts and the time and attention you are willing to give to your chosen career. For many people, working in a pet-related service career is the best job they could ever have hoped for.

chapter 13
OBEDIENCE TRAINER

"Animals learn through repetition and gentle training methods—never through fear," says Obedience Trainer Barbara Long.

Lucy was a friendly, fourteen-month-old golden retriever. She was so excited about meeting people that she greeted them by jumping on them. She needed help with changing this bad habit. Katy was a cheerful, eight-week-old mixed-breed puppy. She needed to learn not to growl at her family. Charlie was a strong, intelligent border collie. His owner was elderly. Charlie needed to learn not to pull on his leash when he and his owner went for walks.

Today, these dogs have overcome their bad habits. What do they all have in common? They are graduates of Paw in Hand, a dog obedience training program run by Barbara Long of Chapel Hill, North Carolina.

A dog can be a wonderful friend. Dogs are naturally loyal and protective, and they willingly give us a furry shoulder to cry on when things go wrong. Even the best of dogs, however, needs training. Like their wild ancestors, dogs are pack animals by nature. They are smart and like to do things with people. This makes them great candidates for learning proper behavior around humans. Yet sometimes people seem to think pets should train themselves. You would not expect a child to say "please" and "thank you" if he or she has never been taught good manners. Likewise, a dog must be taught good manners for living with his or her human family.

A professional obedience trainer teaches pets—usually dogs—how to behave. Even more, he or she teaches people how to communicate with and understand their pets. Barbara calls her dog obedience training business Paw in Hand for a reason. "Training is a team effort," she says. "It is something you do with your dog, not to your dog."

Some people are naturally good at working with animals. Many obedience trainers start out by teaching their own pets to behave. However, a natural talent for working with animals is not enough by itself. Today's dog obedience trainers learn their skills in different ways. For some, college courses lead to a career in obedience training. Others learn obedience training skills while working in law enforcement agencies, animal shelters or the military. Although there are currently no official professional standards for obedience trainers, there are professional organizations individuals can turn to for support and information. Professional groups, humane organizations and educational institutions will all play an important role in developing future standards for this growing profession.

A dog obedience trainer usually leads group classes for dogs and their owners. He or she may also work with individual dogs and owners. Classes may take place at a facility owned by the obedience trainer or at a public building such as a civic center or animal shelter.

"Like people," says Barbara, "all dogs are different. So, they have different problems." Barbara begins by trying to understand each dog and his or her situation. "What is a dog really saying, for instance, when he tears up the sofa? The answer? 'I'm bored,'" she explains. "Most dogs don't have enough to do. Not many dogs are doing what they were bred to do. Destroying furniture is also a way of saying, 'I am anxious and tense because my family pack has gone away.' The biggest reward we can give a dog, other than food, is human contact. And to the dog, sometimes bad contact probably seems better than no contact at all." Training methods always need to be gentle. Animals learn through repetition, not fear, according to Barbara.

"Often people assume an animal understands what they want simply because *they* know what they want. A dog may not understand why it is important to 'sit,' 'come' or 'stay.' Yet a dog can learn to do these things on command through repeated actions," explains Barbara.

Sometimes Barbara plays games with dogs to help them learn. Some of the games involve teaching them to search out a toy or food that she has hidden. In group classes, puppies and owners sometimes perform relay races that incorporate basic commands like "come," "sit" and "down." "Dogs love to play," says Barbara. "Anything that is fun helps them to learn."

In addition to group and individual training classes, Barbara also conducts obedience classes on behalf of her local shelter, the Animal Protection Society of Orange County. Dogs who have received obedience classes are less likely to be returned to the shelter for behavior problems. So the shelter has its own training program, which Barbara teaches.

How did Barbara become an obedience trainer? It all started when she adopted Casey—"the world's worst puppy," according to Barbara. "Casey was the delinquent of the puppy world," she laughs. Barbara took Casey to the dog obedience classes at the shelter. "Every session, we were kept after class to do extra practice," she says. She began learning about training herself so she could work with Casey on her own. It took lots of love, patience and hard work—but today Casey is a wonderful dog and friend.

At the time Barbara was training Casey, she was working as a shelter manager. She felt angry and frustrated with people for giving up their pets. Yet at the same time—having had a dog who was particularly challenging to train—she could also understand some of their feelings.

"I wanted to reach people and their dogs before they got to the point where their problems were that bad," says Barbara. "I knew that once an owner had decided to turn a dog in to the shelter, it was too late. That is why I decided to go into business for myself as a dog trainer." She believes that her experience with Casey, combined with her background as a shelter manager, has given her a special understanding of pets and their problems. "I want to help solve those problems before they reach a crisis point," she explains.

What are the qualities it takes to be a dog obedience trainer? "You need lots of patience," says Barbara. "You also have to enjoy teaching and being with pets and people." If you have these qualities, you might one day find yourself working as a dog obedience trainer, like Barbara Long.

Could You Have a Career as an **Obedience Trainer?**

Do you love being around dogs? Are you the kind of person who can "think like an animal"—that is, understand what makes an animal behave a certain way? If so, a career as an obedience trainer might be right for you. Here are some ideas to explore:

1. Do you love dogs? Then visit the World Wide Web of Dogs at http://www.hsc.usc.edu/~rneville/doglinks.html. There's lots of great information you and your friends will enjoy sharing.

2. If you have a dog of your own, find out about obedience training classes in your area. Some classes offered are just for kids and their dogs. Taking your dog to a training class can help your pet become a better family member and will help you decide whether you would enjoy this kind of work. To receive a list of trainers endorsed by the National Association of Dog Obedience Instructors, write to this organization at 729 Grapevine Hwy., Suite 369, Hurst, TX 76054-2085, or check out their website at http://www.kimberly.uidaho.edu/nadoi/. You can also contact the Association of Pet Dog Trainers, P.O. Box 385, Davis, CA 95617, 800-PET-DOGS. Their website is http://www.APDT.com.

3. If you are interested in becoming a dog obedience trainer, read all you can about the subject. One good book is *Dog Training for Kids* by Carol Lea Benjamin.

chapter 14
PET-SITTER

Professional pet-sitting involves more than just leaving food and water out and then walking out the door, as Pet-Sitter Donna Pease can tell you.

The rewarding world of animal work offers many opportunities for people to create their own careers or start their own businesses. A love of animals, experience, good business skills and an ability to work well with others can result in a unique and personalized career—like that of Donna Pease, a pet-sitter.

For several years, Donna has run her own part-time business, called Tendercare Pet Sitting. For many families, a pet-sitter is as important to having a successful household as a baby-sitter is. A vacation cannot be planned, a business trip cannot be undertaken, until it is certain that a pet-sitter is available. Those who regard dogs, cats and other pets as valued family members understand the importance of caring for pets in the home when the family is away.

"Dogs and cats in particular are more comfortable in their home environment," says Donna. "They may be stressed and irritable in a kennel or boarded at an animal hospital." Who could fully enjoy their vacation knowing that their best canine or feline friend was unhappy?

Professional pet-sitting usually involves more than just putting out food and water and walking out the door. Pets need attention. A conscientious pet-sitter usually expects to spend some time with animal clients. It is important that an animal experiences as little change in routine as possible. As Donna explains, "If I am sitting for someone who routinely watches TV with their cat on their lap, I may spend some time holding the cat, watching television and providing company. With a dog, I might go for a walk, play ball, throw a Frisbee or go for a ride in the car if the owner has approved it earlier in writing."

Before beginning work for a new client, most pet-sitters schedule an interview. It helps a sitter to get to know both the owner and the pet ahead of time. The pet-sitter talks with the owner, meets his or her pet and discusses their routine. Where to walk the dog, how much food to give the pet, what medicine the animal needs, if any—these are all important issues the pet-sitter needs to discuss with the owner. The pet-sitter may ask that the owner sign a contract specifying exactly what the pet-sitter is to do. Such a contract often includes basic information about each pet to be cared for, telephone numbers to call in case of emergency, and other important information.

Like many pet-sitters, Donna does not limit her services to caring for pets. While owners are away she also carries out instructions to water plants, adjust lighting to make the home look occupied, bring in mail or newspapers, and fill bird feeders. "Some owners will take me out on the walk route for their dog or share special instructions for playing with their cat," she explains.

A successful pet-sitter must be prepared for any problems that might arise. He or she should know how to restrain an animal in an emergency situation, and must be physically able to do so. Having a leash or pet carrier on hand is important in case an animal needs to be taken to a veterinarian.

There is no formal educational path for people who want to start their own pet-sitting business. Many pet-sitters develop their skills by caring for their own pets or, as in Donna's case, by working around animals. Donna learned her skills in animal care by working on a farm. Jobs in a variety of office settings helped her develop her business skills.

In addition to a love of animals, the professional pet-sitter must be business-minded about his or her work. It is necessary to keep track of the time spent on each client. In addition, the sitter needs to bill clients, keep track of payments and advertise the business. Although most pet-sitters find running their business very satisfying, it is also a big challenge. As Donna says, "I do it all by myself. It is especially difficult when holidays come around. Then there are more pets to care for than time allows."

Donna's favorite thing about her job is the variety of animals that she encounters. Because she lives in a rural area, she may take care of dogs and cats for one client, and cows, horses and pigs for the next. "There are a number of family farms where I live," explains Donna. "I like going to the farms to see how they are set up. It is interesting to observe the different techniques set up for feeding the animals." She also especially enjoys being recognized and trusted by an animal she has not taken care of for a while.

Donna has some advice for anyone who wants to make a living by taking care of animals. "Learn to communicate with animals," she says. "Some animals require a little more effort than others. You may have to talk to them in a soft, low voice and move slowly and quietly around them before you can get close to them." Her advice about petting animals? "Always ask the owner if it is okay. Then, let the animal meet you. Animals meet one each other by smelling. Before I ever pet an animal, I let the animal get to know me by holding out the back of my hand so he or she can smell it."

Donna helps animals by making sure they stay safe and content while their owners are away. In addition, the service she provides helps the owners by giving them peace of mind about both their animals and their homes. "I don't know if all of the pet owners I work for appreciate all that I do," observes Donna, "but it's important to me to do a good job. I like getting paid for my work, but what is most important are the animals and the time I spend with them." Spending time with animals is the best thing about being a pet-sitter.

Could You Have a Career as a
Pet-Sitter?

Do you love being around pets? Do you have good business skills? Are you a self-starter? Could you run your own business, advertise it and keep track of payments? If so, a career as a pet-sitter might be right for you. Here are some ideas for further exploration:

1. Learn all you can about pets and pet care. Interview pet owners and learn about the different ways they care for their pets. Make a booklet showcasing the different pets in your neighborhood and the care they need.

2. Can't find a summer job? You might consider starting your own dog-walking service for relatives and friends. However, make sure you have your parents' permission, and never enter the home of a stranger.

3. For more information about pet-sitting, contact the National Association of Pet Sitters, 1020 Brookstown Ave., Suite 3, Winston-Salem, NC 27101. This organization offers information for adults, but you and your parents may enjoy sharing it. You can also contact Pet Sitters International, 418 E. King St., King, NC 27021.

chapter 15
PET TAXI DRIVER

Pet Taxi Driver, Larry Reilly, makes sure pets get where they need to go—providing a service to pets and their owners.

© PATTY DENNIS

"Taxi! Taxi!" A young woman and her large German shepherd are standing at the corner of a busy street. She has taken the day off from her office job to take her beloved pet to the veterinarian. She raises her hand to hail a bright yellow cab. The taxi driver pulls up, takes one look at the dog and drives off. What are the woman and her dog to do? They can't miss that appointment!

Getting your pet from one place to another can be difficult. If you don't own a car—and many people in large cities do not—you could have a real problem. Pet owners in New York City, however, have it easy. They can always call Pet Taxi.

Larry Reilly is the owner/driver of Pet Taxi, a cab service for animals. He began his business several years ago. "I was working at another job," says Larry. "As a dog owner, I saw a need for a transportation service. Every time I had to travel with my pet, it was a hassle. There wasn't anyone else running such a business at the time. I thought, 'If there isn't a pet taxi service, there should be.'" Larry had a strong interest in animals and was eager to start a business on his own.

During a typical day, a pet taxi driver takes people and their pets, or the pets alone, to the veterinarian, groomer, kennel or airport. From time to time, he or she may get a call to transport an injured animal to a veterinary hospital. A successful pet taxi driver keeps a stretcher handy in case of emergencies, and must be experienced in handling sick and injured animals.

Larry drives a big yellow van decorated with a "taxi-style" black-and-white checkered band. "When it pulls up, most dogs are excited," he says. "They love riding in the temperature-controlled van." Cats? Most "could take it or leave it," he says. "But we make sure they are secure and comfortable. They don't seem bothered by the ride," he observes. His Pet Taxi van is equipped with animal carriers of all sizes to ensure that animals stay safe during transport.

Sometimes Larry works with breed rescue groups. "These are groups that place a particular breed of dog in good homes," he explains. "I may get a call to transport a boxer, for instance, from an animal shelter to a foster home. All the paperwork has to have been taken care of beforehand by the shelter and the client."

Larry has driven pets to places as far away as Columbus (Ohio), Boston and Philadelphia. "People who work in New York are relocating all the time," he says. "When they take a job in a new city, they may board their pet at a kennel until they have found a place to live. Then they hire me to drive the pet from the kennel to their new home."

Running your own pet-related business can be a wonderful experience. One of the best parts is working with animals and with people who care about animals. In addition, when you control your own business, you decide what hours you will work, when you will take your vacations and how much money you will make. These aspects of being self-employed can be very satisfying.

But running your own business is not all fun, even when your clients are animals. For one thing, as Larry says, "you work harder than ever before." Larry often puts in plenty of ten- to twelve-hour days, six days a week. "I don't think I could have put in such long hours for someone else's business," he says, "but when it is your own business, that's different."

A pet taxi driver needs many things to start a business. First, he or she needs to have at least one van for transporting animals. Although some pets travel in their own carriers, not all owners are prepared. So the pet taxi needs to have animal carriers in a variety of sizes.

Insurance is important in any service business. Both van and driver need to be insured. Many pet taxi drivers are also bonded. This means that the driver posts a certain amount of money as a promise to do his or her job in a responsible way. Many workers who go into people's homes as part of their job are bonded.

It is helpful for pet taxi drivers to have cellular telephones, because they are often outside their offices and need to be able to take calls from potential clients. Finally, there's the business of running a business. Bills must be sent out. Payments and expenses must be kept track of. People need to know about the business and the services it offers, so advertising is important. Pet taxi drivers may start out by doing all the driving themselves. That is what Larry does. If the business does well, the owner may buy more vans and hire more drivers.

Being a pet taxi driver is not always easy. Sometimes Larry gets expensive parking tickets—like when he receives an emergency call and must park in a place where no parking is allowed. There are other challenges too—like when a pet is loose in an owner's apartment, instead of in an animal carrier and ready to travel.

Larry once spent more than an hour trying to catch a cat who needed to be taken to a veterinarian. He was at the home of an elderly gentleman who was confined to a wheelchair. The man's two white cats, Fred and Ginger, looked exactly alike, but Ginger was sick. Because her owner was handicapped, Larry needed to find her and put her in a carrier himself. "The cats were shy," says Larry. "I followed them from room to room. Every time I brought out what I thought was the right cat, the owner told me I had the wrong one." It took a while, but Larry was persistent. He finally caught Ginger and got her to her appointment safely.

Larry is proud that his job makes it much easier for pets and their owners to get where they need to go. "Getting a pet to the groomer or the vet can be stressful in the city," he explains. "My business makes the task easy. I think that is something pet owners appreciate."

Could You Have a Career as a
Pet Taxi Driver?

Do you love pets? Do you like the idea of working for yourself—instead of for somebody else? Running your own pet-related business is a challenge, but it just might be right for you. Here are some suggestions for further exploration:

1. Do you have what it takes to run your own business? Make a list of the characteristics that a self-employed person should have. For instance, such a person needs to be trustworthy, responsible, organized, and good at responding to unexpected problems or challenges. Next, think of a time when you demonstrated each characteristic you have listed.

2. Find out more about the pet taxi business by writing to the Independent Pet and Animal Transportation Association, P.O. Box 129, Arvada, CO 80001.

part four
Careers Working with Wildlife

From the peregrine falcon roosting on a skyscraper to the raccoon who checks out your trash can at night, wild animals are all around us. The world of work offers many career opportunities for helping and protecting wild animals. Some people make their living studying animals in the wild. Or they may work to protect the places where wild animals live—their habitats. Other individuals educate the public about wild animals. Still others may heal sick or injured wild animals and release them back into their natural habitats. Wild animals belong in the wild. They should never be thought of or treated as "pets." But what happens when wild animals are in trouble? They may need a little temporary help. In that case, people who are trained to work with wildlife can help.

Different Ways to Work with Wildlife

Wildlife workers may help animals directly, as in the case of a wildlife rehabilitator or wildlife veterinarian who cares for sick, injured or orphaned animals. Studying animals humanely can also provide benefits to wildlife. When people understand more about animals, they are more likely to appreciate them and not harm them through ignorance. A naturalist at a nature center may help animals just by teaching the public to respect the natural areas where wild animals live.

A person who is interested in working with wildlife needs to have a deep commitment to animals and the environment. Some jobs involve working outdoors. When the weather is nice, this can be a pleasure. When it is cold and wet, the job still needs to be done. But not all work with wild animals is done outdoors. Some jobs involve working in an office as an administrator, writer or educator.

The Work of the Wildlife Biologist

Most wildlife biologists specialize in studying a particular group or kind of animal, such as bats, birds or mammals. They combine years of education with practical work in the field, which may involve observing, counting or "banding" (marking for identification purposes) the kind of animal they are studying. Working with animals in the wild takes patience and hard work. Often, study projects involving animals are conducted over long periods of time. The people involved in these projects need to be willing to take on long-term work and stick with it.

For the young person interested in a career in wildlife biology, science classes are important—especially classes in biology and environmental studies. Most wildlife biologists have an undergraduate degree (usually in biology) as well as a graduate degree—a master's or a doctorate. In addition, depending on where the wildlife biologist works, he or she may need to take special training or pass certain exams. He or she may also need a license to work with a particular kind of animal—especially if that kind of animal is rare or endangered.

Talking to the Animals

Like the wildlife biologist, the animal communication specialist makes a career out of studying animals. He or she may study animals in the wild or in an indoor research setting. And also like the wildlife biologist, the animal communication specialist must have qualities of patience and dedication to animals. Research may be conducted over a period of months or years, so the ability to stick to a project once it is begun is important.

The animal communication specialist starts out with a strong background in the sciences—with an emphasis in biology. The researcher in animal communication is also likely to have an undergraduate degree (usually in biology) and a graduate degree—a master's or a doctorate. The study of animal communication is a highly specialized field. Yet as the public becomes more interested in the creatures with whom we share our world, opportunities in this line of work are sure to increase.

The Healing Arts

People who work directly with wild animals include those who help sick, injured and orphaned wildlife, such as the marine mammal stranding specialist and the wildlife rehabilitator. A person who pursues this kind of work must be strongly dedicated to animals. The work often takes place at a nonprofit organization. Preparation usually includes a background in the sciences. An understanding of the needs and behavior of animals is also important. Caring responsibly for a pet can be a good way to start developing this kind of understanding.

Depending on where they work, the marine mammal stranding specialist and the wildlife rehabilitator may be required to have first-aid training. Some centers that care for wildlife rely on outside veterinarians or veterinary technicians. Most people who work in this area are employed by government or nonprofit organizations whose goal is to help wild animals.

Helping Animals by Teaching People

The skills and experience of the naturalist or environmental educator and the wildlife refuge manager are alike in some ways. Individuals who pursue these jobs must be dedicated to preserving the environment, and educating the public usually plays an important role in both jobs.

Although the naturalist's job does not routinely involve handling wild animals, he or she does observe native wildlife in the field. Teaching others about these animals and the places where they live is also an important task. Most naturalists work for nonprofit agencies whose goal is to teach the public about animals and the environment. Naturalists and environmental educators usually have an undergraduate degree in the natural sciences, environmental management, or education. They may also have a graduate degree—a master's or a doctorate.

The wildlife refuge manager usually works for a nonprofit or government organization. Many wildlife refuges are maintained by federal and state agencies. The training for jobs in federal and state refuges is often somewhat different from that required at privately owned and maintained refuges. Many refuge managers who work for government agencies must have an undergraduate degree and experience in law enforcement or conservation. Both state and federal governments, however, have strict educational requirements for all job offerings. Before seriously considering a career with a government agency, you need to learn more about the requirements for specific jobs.

Like the naturalist, the manager of a private, nonprofit wildlife refuge is likely to have an educational background that includes training and experience in the natural sciences, environmental management, or education. Also like the naturalist, the wildlife refuge manager may have a master's degree in one of these subjects as well. He or she may also need a license or permit that allows the handling of wild animals in emergency situations.

Good observation skills are important for the wildlife refuge manager, as is a love of working outdoors. The manager of a privately owned refuge often directs (or in some cases performs) the work of maintaining the refuge. He or she may conduct educational and fundraising efforts. Keeping careful, detailed records of animals and plants and their survival in the refuge is also important.

Choosing Your Career

If you love the outdoors and have a strong concern for animals and the environment, an exciting job working with wildlife may be right for you. Ask yourself some basic questions: Would you rather go walking in the woods than skateboarding in the city? Would you be happy spending long periods of time watching wild animals go about their daily routines? Do you feel a commitment to the environment? Are you the kind of person who can commit to a long-term project and stick with it? Your answers to these questions should give you a general idea whether a career working with wildlife might be right for you.

chapter 16
WILDLIFE BIOLOGIST

Dr. Merlin Tuttle has devoted his life to protecting bats all over the world through his organization, Bat Conservation International.

You are standing outside a cave in the desert. Night is just beginning to fall. Suddenly, the air is filled with bats. Thousands of them cover the sky in a dark cloud of rapidly beating wings. They are leaving the cave to hunt for insects. This might seem like a nightmare to someone who does not understand or appreciate these unique animals. But it is a dream come true for Dr. Merlin Tuttle. He is a wildlife biologist and the founder of Bat Conservation International (BCI), based in Austin, Texas.

Bats are flying mammals. They have a furry body and wings. Merlin has spent a lifetime studying them in the wild. As the founder of an international nonprofit organization, however, he does more than just study these misunderstood animals. He also works to protect bats and their habitats around the world. He does this by writing, speaking, establishing local programs and educating people.

For example, take the time when the city planners of Austin decided to remodel one of the city's bridges. Before the work began, the Congress Avenue Bridge was home to only a few bats. Afterward, bats moved in by the tens of thousands. It seemed that the newly remodeled bridge provided a very good bat home. But the citizens of Austin were frightened. Many wanted the bats removed.

That's when Merlin stepped in. Through him and his organization, the people of Austin learned the truth about bats. They discovered that bats play a very important role. In a single night, the Austin bats can eat up to thirty thousand pounds of insects, many of which would otherwise harm people or crops. The city of Austin learned to appreciate its bats. Today, theirs is the largest bat colony in a North American city. People come from all around to watch the bats take flight. It is a fascinating sight to watch more than one million bats spiral into the night sky!

A successful wildlife biologist like Dr. Merlin Tuttle is patient and has good observation skills. He or she needs to be comfortable working outdoors in all kinds of weather. Taking careful, detailed notes is vital to this line of work. A person who decides to pursue this career will need to get a graduate degree—a master's or a doctorate. That involves many years of undergraduate and postgraduate study.

Many wildlife biologists also believe it is important for them to help people understand the roles that wild animals play in nature. When people appreciate how all the animals and plants in an ecosystem work together, they are more likely to give animals and their habitats the respect and protection they need.

As a child, Merlin knew what he wanted to do when he grew up. His parents were interested in natural history, and he became interested as well. At age five he was watching birds, butterflies, snakes and amphibians. When he was nine, his parents began taking him to natural history museums, where Merlin introduced himself to the museum curators. They were impressed with how much he knew about wildlife.

As a teenager, Merlin became interested in studying gray bats. He observed the bats and began collecting information that he would one day use to earn his doctoral degree. "In those days, all the books said that gray bats did not migrate. It was believed they lived in one cave year-round. At age sixteen, I went to the Smithsonian

Institution," he says. "I told curators there that I believed the gray bats *did* migrate. At the Smithsonian, they listened. They gave me one thousand numbered bat bands and told me to place the bands on the bats and see where they went."

Tracking the gray bats was not easy. It meant traveling through remote areas. It meant climbing into dark caves. It meant crossing steep cliffs by rope. "Within three months," says Merlin, "I had found the place where the bats hibernated—one hundred miles north of where I lived." It was a startling discovery—and all the more unusual because it was made by a young person. "One is never too young to start making such observations," says Merlin. "Anyone can make a discovery that is new to science."

Merlin received special training to do the work he did. He agrees who young people should never touch a wild animal—especially a bat. A bat who is lying on the ground may be sick and could bite you. If you see an injured animal, always find an adult to help.

It is easy to see how Merlin's work helps bats. Does his work help people too? Merlin thinks so. "I have found that often what we do to help wildlife and the environment is extremely helpful to people as well," he explains.

How does learning about and protecting animals help people? Bats are a good example. When bats thrive, flowers are well pollinated. This means the plants produce more fruit. When the plants thrive, the people who earn their living by selling plant products also prosper. And larger animals that eat fruit have more to eat and thrive as well.

Some bats pollinate plants. Others eat insects that eat crops. Thousands of insects may be eaten in one night. Farmers often use chemical pesticides to destroy insects on their crops. But relying on bats and other natural predators is safer for the environment. Bats do not cause chemical pollution, which saves farmers time and money. When bats are allowed to help control insects, everybody benefits. Merlin believes that the key to protecting the environment lies in working together. "We need to learn to work with other people. Even if we may disagree on some ideas, we must learn to listen and reach a compromise."

Merlin is proud of his work with Bat Conservation International. When he first presented his idea for a bat protection group, most people thought he would not succeed. They thought that nobody would support an organization to help bats. "Today we have fourteen thousand members in seventy-six countries," he says. "And we have protected many of the world's most important bat caves and other habitats." Through his work as a wildlife biologist, Dr. Merlin Tuttle has shown that protecting these flying mammals isn't just good for the bats themselves. It is good for people and the environment too.

© MERLIN D. TUTTLE

Relying on bats and other natural predators to control insects is safer for the environment than using chemical pesticides.

Could You Have a Career as a Wildlife Biologist?

A person who is interested in becoming a wildlife biologist should have a strong background in science. Patience and good observation skills are also important. As a child, wildlife biologist Dr. Jane Goodall once spent six hours watching a hen to understand the process of laying an egg. If you have this kind of patience, a career in wildlife biology might be right for you. Here are some ideas for further exploration:

1. Find out more about wildlife biology by getting to know the people who work at a local natural history museum. Or, e-mail a wildlife biologist who works at a museum or wildlife agency in your state.

2. Learn more about the work done by wildlife biologists at Bat Conservation International, the organization founded by Dr. Merlin Tuttle. Write to them at P.O. Box 162603, Austin, TX 78716, or visit their website at http://www.batcon.org/. BCI offers a slide program that you can use to teach others about protecting bats.

3. Read about and observe wild animals. Get to know your native wildlife. Ask your teacher if you can do a science project that involves watching wildlife. While you're at it, read more about Dr. Merlin Tuttle's work in *Batman: Exploring the World of Bats* by Lawrence Pringle. Check for it at your school or public library.

Chapter 17
ANIMAL COMMUNICATION SPECIALIST

The Fouts are a husband-and-wife team who has made the study of animal communication their life's work.

© APRIL OTTEY

What if animals could talk? What would a toucan tell you about the rain forest? What would a sea turtle say about life in the ocean? If you've ever wanted to talk to the animals, you would enjoy meeting Roger and Deborah Fouts. They have made talking with animals their life's work.

Let's visit Roger and Deborah at their workplace. Ready? First, crouch low to the ground. Now, make your way inside. Sound a little strange? It might—if Roger and Deborah worked in an office. Their workplace, however, is the Chimpanzee and Human Communication Institute at Central Washington University. Crouching low to the ground as you enter is a little like saying, "I am not a threat" in the language of chimpanzees. And, if you visit the Foutses, you'll need to learn to talk chimp!

Dr. Roger Fouts and Deborah Fouts are scientists who study animal communication. They have spent years teaching chimpanzees to use sign language. Their research has helped people better understand communication—both human and chimpanzee.

Let's meet their co-workers. Washoe is the oldest chimp. Roger began working with her more than thirty years ago, when he was a graduate student. Washoe was taught to use American Sign Language (ASL). In ASL, people form signs with their hands. The signs represent words and ideas. For example, tapping the tips of the fingers of both hands together is the sign for MORE.

In the wild, chimpanzees are very social animals. They use body language and hand movements to communicate. They also make special noises that show how they feel. Chimpanzees cannot talk like humans, but they certainly can communicate.

In her first four years of learning sign language, Washoe learned more than one hundred signs. Today she knows many more. She routinely uses sign language to tell Roger, Deborah and others what she is thinking and feeling. She signs COOKIE when she wants her favorite treat. She signs NO when a graduate student tries to get her to take part in a dull experiment. She even makes up signs of her own, like WATER BIRD for "swan" or CANDY DRINK for "watermelon."

Washoe lives with four other adopted chimps—Dar, Tatu, Moja and Loulis. They live in an "apartment" of room-sized cages connected by walkways. In many ways, they are a lot like human children. They enjoy treats. They like being hugged. They love looking at pictures in books and magazines and playing with toys. Moja especially enjoys the sound that Velcro makes when pulled apart.

Roger and Deborah arrive early each morning. The chimps are already awake. Signed conversations start right away with morning greetings. Next the graduate students arrive. The Foutses oversee their research in animal communication. Many scientists who study animal communication conduct their studies outdoors. They have to go to the animals' natural habitats in the wild and observe and record their communication in all kinds of weather. But researchers at the Chimpanzee and Human Communication Institute have it easy. They do all their observations in the chimp enclosure.

To start the day, everyone eats breakfast. At the institute, the people and the chimps eat the same foods—this morning, a fruit smoothie with vitamins and pieces of fruit. The motto at mealtimes is "If you wouldn't eat it, don't give it to a chimp."

After breakfast, it is time for work and play. "Captive animals do not have a lot of control over their environment," says Deborah. "So we try to make the chimps' two large activity areas as interesting as possible." There are fire hoses for the chimps to swing on, cargo nets for them to play in or lie on, and objects for them for climb on.

The students doing animal communication research observe the chimps and practice signing to them. They take notes on the chimps' responses. "The chimps choose what to do and where to go within the enclosures," says Deborah. "Humans have to go where the chimps decide. If a student wants to do research and a chimp wants to play, they play," she explains. "Chimps come first here."

Some scientists say that animals do not communicate. They say that Washoe and the other chimps have not really learned sign language. They think the chimps have just learned tricks to get what they want. Roger has an answer to this. He says that in experiments with Washoe and the other chimps, food is not used just as a reward for correct signing. Roger signs to the chimps about many things besides food and treats. And, the Foutses have videotaped the chimps signing to each other when no humans were around.

Washoe has shown in many ways that she understands the signs she uses. She can apply the meaning of a sign to more than one object or situation. Some signs always mean the same thing—like APPLE. But a sign like OPEN can apply to many things—a door, a cage or a can of food. Washoe has shown that she can use the sign OPEN and apply it to all these items. In addition, Washoe has taught Loulis to communicate using the sign language that was taught to her.

The Foutses believe that good science, like friendship, is about commitment and caring. This is why they make sure that the chimps' days are full of activity and companionship. Through their organization Friends of Washoe, the Foutses also work to protect other chimpanzees—both in the wild and in captivity. They support projects that save habitats for wild chimpanzees. And they campaign to discourage people from capturing chimps from the wild.

How does a person get involved in animal studies that do not harm the animals? "It can be hard when you are starting out," says Deborah, "because not everyone will share your views on what is humane. I think you have to refuse to dissect for a start. Years ago, people did not feel empowered to do that. But now, more people realize that they have a choice."

Many researchers in animal communication start out in the field of ethology. Ethology is the study of how animals behave. Ethologists study animals in their natural habitats in the wild. Today, animal communication studies are being conducted with many different kinds of animals. Researchers are studying the songs of whales, the low-frequency sounds that elephants make to signal each other, and the use of sign language with gorillas, to name a few projects. If you love animals and science, you too may one day be able to talk with the animals!

Could You Have a Career as an Animal Communication Specialist?

Interested in this exciting scientific career? If so, you need to have strong science skills. You also need to have the personal characteristics of any good scientist—patience, persistence and discipline. Here are some ideas to help you decide whether a career as an animal communication specialist might be right for you:

1. If you know someone who has a career in the sciences—whether he or she works with animals or atoms—talk to that person. Find out what qualities and skills a successful scientist needs.

2. If you are interested in animal communication, learn more about the work of Dr. Roger Fouts and Deborah Fouts at the Chimpanzee and Human Communication Institute at Central Washington University. Write to them at Friends of Washoe, P.O. Box 728, Ellensburg, WA 98926, or visit their website at http://www.cwu.edu/~cwuchci.

3. Read about animals and how they communicate. One good book is *Signs of the Apes, Songs of the Whales: Adventures in Human-Animal Communication* by George Harrar and Linda Harrar (New York: Simon & Schuster, 1989). Also, read the chapter on Katharine Payne and her work with elephant communication in *EcoWomen: Protectors of the Earth* by Willow Ann Sirch (Golden, CO: Fulcrum Publishing).

chapter 18
MARINE MAMMAL STRANDING SPECIALIST

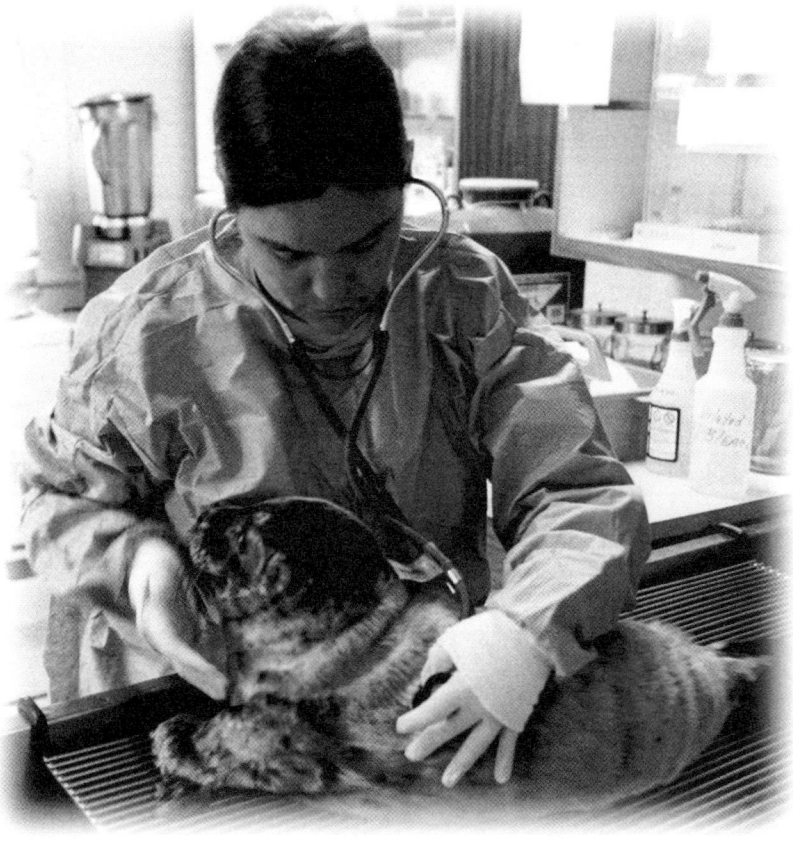

Marine Mammal Stranding Specialist Dawn Smith examines an injured seal at the Marine Mammal Center in Sausalito, California.

It was early morning. The baby harbor seal was all alone at the edge of the rocky shore. The waves washed over his small, brown body. He shook himself helplessly and gazed out into the bay as if looking for his lost parent. The mother seal was nowhere to be found. Minutes later, an early morning beachcomber discovered the small furry youngster. Fortunately, he knew what to do.

"There's a baby seal stranded on the beach. Please tell me how I can help." That's the kind of call that Dawn Smith, a marine mammal stranding specialist,

often receives at the Marine Mammal Center in Sausalito, California. A wildlife rehabilitator helps sick, injured and orphaned wild animals, and Dawn is a special kind of wildlife rehabilitator. She works only with marine mammals. Last year, Dawn and other staff members at the Marine Mammal Center treated nearly eight hundred animals, including seals, sea lions, whales, dolphins and sea otters.

What is it like to work at one of the largest and most unusual animal hospitals in the world? "It's challenging," says Dawn. "Treating marine mammals is more difficult, in some ways, than treating other wildlife. There is so much we don't know about their life in the wild. We are just now learning how deep these animals can dive, how long they can stay underwater. There's still a lot more to learn—but the challenge is also what makes it fun."

Some marine mammal stranding specialists are veterinarians. Some are trained as veterinary technicians. Dawn is a veterinary technician whose career began with two years of study in a veterinary technician program at a junior college. Then she took an exam to be able to work in her field. After ten years of working with companion animals, she changed jobs and began her work with marine mammals at the Marine Mammal Center.

A marine mammal stranding specialist's day starts early. Work begins with a look at all the patients who were kept overnight. This gives the marine mammal stranding specialist an idea of which animals need to be treated right away. Just like in a hospital for humans, every patient at the Marine Mammal Center has a medical chart. The chart is a record of the animal's illness or injury and the treatment received. The marine mammal stranding specialist reviews the chart for each animal. If there has been a change in an animal's condition, the specialist may have to make immediate changes in the animal's feeding, medicine or housing.

As a veterinary technician, Dawn conducts physical exams and takes blood samples. She administers medicine and treats some injuries. She also decides what the animals will eat and how they will be housed. She works closely with a veterinarian to give each animal the best care possible.

Gill and Van Gogh were two young sea lions found tangled in fishing net. "We see entangled animals fairly often—mostly sea lions like Gill and Van Gogh," says Dawn. This is because sea lions feed on the same type of fish that fishers set their nets on. Often, the sea lions are strong enough to break out of the net itself, but come away with a "necklace" of netting. "We take them in, remove the netting, and give them medication and time to heal. Then we release them. Animals can be harmed by human actions," adds Dawn. "That is why it is important to obey laws about where people can set nets and fishing lines." The laws have changed since Gill and Van Gogh were rescued. People can no longer set gill nets in the area where the two sea lions were found.

A marine mammal stranding specialist may work with volunteers. About seven hundred volunteers work at the Marine Mammal Center over the course of a single year! These volunteers do much more than stuff envelopes. They perform a large amount of the actual work with the animals. The volunteers are organized into crews of eight or more who work as a team and are led by a supervisor. Each volunteer makes a commitment to work at least once a week.

The volunteers undergo a special medical training program. Dawn and other marine mammal specialists teach them how to restrain an animal, set up an IV, and give medicine, including injections. They also teach the volunteers about emergency medical care.

Working in teams is important when you are dealing with marine mammals. With a 250-pound sea lion, Dawn may need up to five volunteers just to hold the animal. Speed is important. "Our goal is to go in, do what needs to be done and get out as quickly as possible to reduce the stress on our wild patient," she explains.

What happens when someone calls in to say they have found a stranded marine mammal? Dawn may talk to the caller to determine the animal's needs. Is the animal really sick or hurt? If not, the animal needs to be left alone. "Sometimes a pup is found on the beach by itself, but the mother is nearby," she explains. For instance, harbor seal mothers forage at dusk and dawn and may leave a pup on a deserted beach.

"Perhaps," says Dawn, "when the mother left her baby, there was no one on the beach. Then someone comes along and finds the pup. The worst thing they can do is to pick the pup up. The best thing they can do is to call us. When I get such a call, I tell the person to observe the baby. If a pup is awake and makes noise, that pup has probably been fed recently. His mom won't come back if there are dogs or people in view."

One of the hardest things about working as a marine mammal stranding specialist is having to see animals that have been harmed by human actions. When the Exxon Valdez oil spill occurred, for instance, Dawn went to Alaska. She helped set up a station to treat oiled sea otters. She often worked twelve- to fourteen-hour days. It was a difficult time.

Being a marine mammal stranding specialist is challenging. But there are also many rewards. Seeing that sick or injured marine mammals are cared for and, when possible, released back into the wild, is a thrill. In addition, many specialists like Dawn train volunteers and educate the public about marine mammals. They hope that the public will learn to appreciate these remarkable creatures and come to understand the importance of protecting the oceans and the animals who live there.

Shown here is one of the many faces aided by the Marine Mammal Center.

© MARINE MAMMAL CENTER

Marine Mammal Stranding Specialist

Could You Have a Career as a Marine Mammal Stranding Specialist?

Do you love whales and dolphins? Would you like to work with seals and sea otters? If so, you need strong science skills. You also need to understand how wild animals differ from pets. For instance, pets like to be comforted by the touch of a human hand. Not so with wild animals. They are stressed by human contact. Here are some ideas to help you learn more about the fascinating work of the marine mammal stranding specialist:

1. Learn more about marine mammals and their habitats by writing to the Marine Mammal Center, Marin Headlands, Golden Gate National Recreation Area, Sausalito, CA 94965. Or check out their website at http://www.tmmc.org/ (and hear a seal bark while you're at it!).

2. Talk to a local wildlife rehabilitator or a veterinary technician who works with wildlife and find out all you can about this career.

chapter 19
WILDLIFE REHABILITATOR

Dr. Len Soucy helps injured hawks, owls and other raptors at The Raptor Trust in Millington, New Jersey.

© THE RAPTOR TRUST

It was just a plain old cardboard shoe box—the kind that had once held a pair of sneakers. It was lying on the doorstep. From inside the box came a muffled sound, then silence. On the top was taped a note with two words written on it—Please Help.

The front door of the house opened. A man stepped out onto the doorstep. He spotted the box, brought it indoors and carefully raised the lid. Inside was an alert, fluffy red-tailed hawk chick. Some people would have been surprised to find a shoe box containing a live baby raptor (a hawk, owl or other bird of prey) at their front door. But not Dr. Len Soucy, founder and president of the Raptor Trust in Millington, New Jersey. "Actually, quite a few of our patients come to us in shoe boxes," he observes.

For three decades, the Raptor Trust has provided a safe place for wild hawks, owls and other birds. At this modern wildlife rehabilitation center, injured, sick and orphaned wild birds find food, shelter and healing. Whenever possible, they are released back into the wild.

As the founder of this unique rehabilitation center and a wildlife rehabilitator himself, Len performs many different tasks. His job includes anything and everything that might help animals—from building a large flight enclosure to treating an injured bird. He is not above cleaning a cage or pushing a broom. He also raises the money that keeps the Raptor Trust operating—and it takes plenty of cash to feed, house and care for all those sick and injured wild birds. You might think that Len's career is more varied than that of most wildlife rehabilitators. In fact, it is not that uncommon for a wildlife rehabilitator to find him- or herself performing a wide variety of tasks.

Wildlife rehabilitators need special training. They may get that training in veterinary school or veterinary technician training programs or through special courses of study. They learn how to treat wildlife injuries and diseases. They may learn other special skills as well, like how to create a physical therapy program for a particular kind of animal.

A wildlife rehabilitator must be good at recognizing and treating all kinds of injuries. At the Raptor Trust, the most common injury is the impact injury—when a raptor hits something during flight. Some of these birds fly at high speeds. Peregrine falcons, for example, may dive at speeds of up to 180 miles per hour.

"Raptors can be severely injured or even killed by flying into high-tension wires," says Len. "Glass is another problem. Plenty of birds that fly slowly are injured by flying into windows. Cars are also dangerous. An owl may be hit by a passing car while chasing a mouse across a road. These are the kinds of injuries we see most often," he explains.

Some wildlife rehabilitators also focus strongly on educating the public about ways to avoid injuring wildlife. For instance, Len and his staff do their best to educate any person who brings a raptor to the Raptor Trust. "I tell people not to keep bird feeders so close to the windows of their homes," says Len. "People tend to do that so they can watch wild birds at the feeder from indoors. Yet if a hawk chases a songbird that has come to the feeder, both the hawk and the songbird may end up hitting a glass window. It is best to place bird feeders out in the yard near bushes or shrubs," he advises.

How did Len get his start in wildlife rehabilitation? Years ago, he and his wife, Diane, decided to take a weekend trip. They went to a special place in Pennsylvania called Hawk Mountain. They had heard that this was a great spot for watching migrating hawks in the fall. They did not realize they were about to experience a life-changing event.

On a sunny day, high on Hawk Mountain, they watched as hundreds of wild hawks soared on the currents of warm air that rose from the earth. The hawks were using those air currents to climb high into the skies, flying effortlessly on their journey to a milder climate for the winter. In three days, Len and Diane saw thousands of hawks of all kinds—red-tailed hawks, Cooper's hawks, sharp-shinned hawks and kestrels, to name a few.

Upon returning home to New Jersey, Len realized that he had developed a deep concern for the birds he had seen. In those days, there was no legal protection for hawks and owls. To many people they were pests. Few were interested in protecting them—let alone caring for them when they were injured, sick or orphaned.

Len began treating injured hawks part-time in the backyard of his fourteen-acre property. As people learned about what he was doing, more birds were brought to him. Before long, the project became so large and expensive that he and his family could no longer run it alone.

The Raptor Trust was established as a nonprofit organization in 1982. Today it includes a hospital, an education building, a gift shop and seventy large outdoor cages. There are five full-time staff members. In a single day, 100 birds may be admitted and more than one hundred telephone calls answered. Dozens of volunteers help with the enormous task of feeding and caring for the many birds who are sheltered here until they are healthy enough for release back into the wild. The Raptor Trust specializes in helping hawks and owls; no injured bird of any species, however, is turned away.

Len has some advice for young readers who love animals. "Understand the natural world around you," he says. "Be interested. Be nosy. Turn off your computer and get to know the natural world. The thing to understand about nature is that you do not own it and you cannot control it, but you are a living part of it. There is no need to ask, 'What good are hawks?' 'What good are snakes?' Everything on this Earth is interrelated and important to the whole," he says. That is just the kind of statement you might expect to hear from a committed wildlife rehabilitator like Len Soucy.

© THE RAPTOR TRUST

"If you want to help animals, learn more about the natural world around you," advises Dr. Len Soucy, director of The Raptor Trust.

Could You Have a Career as a Wildlife Rehabilitator?

What does it take to become a wildlife rehabilitator? You need to be calm, caring and strong to help animals in distress. You need to keep in mind that the animal's eventual release back into the wild is your goal. To learn more, explore these ideas:

1. Become the resident wild animal expert in your neighborhood. People often experience difficulties or challenges in dealing with wild animals that live near their homes. The solution may be a simple one. One good way to find out more is to read the book *Wild Neighbors: The Humane Approach to Living with Wildlife, from the Humane Society of the United States.* Look for it at your public library or local bookstore. Although it is written for adults, you and your parents will enjoy sharing it.

2. Tell your friends how important it is never to touch a wild animal—but instead to find an adult to help. Often, the best way to help a wild animal is to leave it alone. Contact a wildlife rehabilitator, wildlife veterinarian or environmental educator at a local nature center for more specific advice about helping wild animals.

3. Find out more about the work of the Raptor Trust by writing to them at 1390 White Bridge Rd., Millington, NJ 07946.

chapter 20
NATURALIST

Naturalist Lori Paradis Brant helps children to understand the importance of protecting animals by preserving the places where animals live.

It was a beautiful day. The sun was shining. The air was scented with pine. A line of about twenty children were obediently following a young woman along a forest trail. Suddenly one little girl stopped walking and began to cry. The woman rushed to her side. "What's wrong?" she asked kindly. The little girl did not answer. "It's the trees," the girl's friend explained. "She has never seen such big trees. She's afraid of them."

Careers *with* Animals

As a naturalist, Lori Paradis Brant teaches children and adults from all different backgrounds to appreciate wild animals and the places where they live. "For an inner-city child who has little experience around nature, even trees can be scary," she observes. Lori is a naturalist and environmental educator at the Connecticut Audubon Society in Fairfield, Connecticut.

"We were walking through our 162-acre sanctuary when this little girl became frightened," Lori explains. "She held my hand tightly for the remainder of our walk. As she listened and began to touch—first, the bark of the trees, then a flower and later a blue jay's feather that we found—she began to be less afraid. By the end of the hike, she was walking by herself, eagerly watching for birds and other sanctuary animals. It felt very rewarding to help her overcome her fear and learn to appreciate nature," says Lori.

Many naturalists work at nature centers, working closely with people of all ages to help them appreciate animals and the environment. Some naturalists work instead for regional or national organizations that work to protect animals and the earth. The naturalist's job may also be found in a government agency—in wildlife management, for instance. A naturalist may serve as the manager of a wildlife refuge or may conduct research on a particular species of animal, similar to the work of a wildlife biologist.

A naturalist needs to be comfortable working with the public. He or she often leads hikes in unspoiled, natural areas and teaches participants about wild animals and plants that live there. One of the rewards for many naturalists comes from helping people appreciate the birds and other wild animals that live nearby. "Often, people don't realize that what they have at home can be every bit as intriguing and exciting as the animals and plants found in an exotic habitat like a rain forest!" Lori emphasizes.

Good telephone skills are important, because most nature centers handle a wide range of nature-related questions by phone. People often call in with questions about feeding birds, identifying wild animals, and gardening with plants that attract butterflies and other creatures. Most naturalists who work to educate the public need to know a great deal about a wide variety of nature topics.

In addition to teaching at the nature center where she works, Lori teaches at schools throughout the state. Much of her teaching is about wild animals. "Animals are an important part of the environment," she says. "I want people to understand that we need to respect wild animals and the places where they live." At the same time, people are an important part of the environment too—because they can change the environment through their actions. "Part of my job is also to try to help people develop a sense of responsibility for nature," says Lori.

Like many naturalists, Lori teaches nature programs for classroom students. Depending on the age group she is working with, in her teaching she might use puppets, photographs, posters, plastic models of animals, real molted feathers, shed snake skins, cast-off shells, or fossils.

Although Lori's school programs are conducted inside a classroom, her programs at the nature center take place both indoors and outside. At the sanctuary where Lori works, people have the opportunity to observe examples of six different kinds of animal habitats. The sanctuary includes an upland forest, a stream, a marsh, a pond, inland wetlands, and hills and meadows.

"Before children enter the sanctuary," Lori says, "I talk with them about how to behave around wildlife. Some children need to be taught not to crush insects or earthworms. Others need to learn not to frighten away ducks and other animals. I try to teach children that visiting the sanctuary is like being a guest in someone else's home—the animals'."

Lori also teaches children that wild animals are not the same as pets. "I teach that wild animals belong in the wild," she says. "If someone sees a box turtle crossing the road, I want them to help that turtle get across the street safely—not put him in their car and take him home. Leaving wild animals in their natural habitat is good for the animals as well as the environment."

As a child, Lori took camping vacations with her family. Her camping experiences helped inspire her love of natural history and her respect for wildlife. Later, while working as a teaching assistant during her college years, she discovered how much she enjoyed educating others. She decided to major in natural science and environmental interpretation.

Like Lori, many naturalists have an undergraduate degree in biology, natural science or education. Those who want to work in a management-oriented job (such as the director of a nature center) may also have a master's degree in environmental management or a related field. The job market for natural history–related careers is very competitive. Persistence and a strong volunteer background can help in landing the right job.

What does Lori like least about her job? At the nature center, she receives calls from people who no longer want the animals they bought at pet stores. "People buy iguanas, for instance, when they are small and cute—not realizing that they can grow to be fifteen feet long. They contact us, hoping we will take the animals off their hands," says Lori, "but we are not able to do that."

Working outdoors is one of the things Lori likes best about her job. "I get to spend a large part of my day outside with nature and the wild animals that I love—and I get to share that love with others. What could be better?"

Could You Have a Career as a Naturalist?

Are you fascinated by wild animals? Is a hike in the woods your idea of fun? Do you feel a strong commitment to protecting the environment? If you love working with others, a job teaching people about natural history might be very rewarding for you. Here are some ideas for further exploration:

1. Find out more about the wild animals that live in your area. Practice using a field guide to identify birds and other creatures.

2. Start a nature journal. Each time you go for a walk in the wild, keep a list of all the animals you see, as well as any evidence of animals—feathers, scat (animal droppings) or empty nut hulls, for instance. Try to identify animals by the evidence they have left behind. Share your discoveries about animals and their habitats with your family and friends.

3. Talk to a naturalist who works at a local nature center, organization or government agency. Also, go online and check out the websites of the environmental protection organizations and agencies in your state.

chapter 21
WILDLIFE REFUGE MANAGER

Managing the Unexpected Wildlife Refuge is a rewarding challenge for Hope Sawyer Buyukmihci.

© DAVE STAUFFER

You are standing at the edge of a beautiful pond surrounded by trees. A large mound of sticks and branches is at one edge of the water. It is a beaver lodge. Is it empty? Suddenly a furry head pops out. Nope—this lodge is *active*!

Discovering an active beaver lodge is something to celebrate. Why? "Because beavers create habitat for all kinds of forest creatures," says Hope Sawyer Buyukmihci.

Hope is the manager of Unexpected Wildlife Refuge, a privately owned nature preserve in Newfield, New Jersey. She and her family bought the land and moved here more than forty years ago.

While Hope's husband pursued his job as a scientist working with metals, Hope spent her days raising a family, taking care of the refuge and observing wildlife. She gave educational talks for clubs, school groups and churches. "In those days, people did not think much about the loss of natural areas," she says. Hope tried to change that. She explained the importance of leaving some land untouched for wild animals. She also shared her fascinating experiences watching beavers at Unexpected Wildlife Refuge and taught people about the importance of these intriguing animals.

How did Hope become so interested in beavers? At first there were few beavers to be found at Unexpected Wildlife Refuge. So many had been killed for their fur that they were almost extinct in New Jersey. But Hope discovered a beaver family at the refuge. She spent long hours observing what they ate, how they built their lodges and how they behaved around other animals. The beavers were fascinating to watch! Hope was amazed at how affectionate the parents were in caring for their young. She also noticed that the "teenagers" helped out with raising the little ones.

Hope learned that the beavers' favorite wild treat was twigs from the poplar tree. She gathered poplar twigs from areas where the beavers did not often go. Then she placed the twigs where the beavers would find them. With a ready food supply, the beaver family did well. In time, the beavers came to expect and even welcome her visits. They even brought their babies, called kits, to greet her. The babies grew up to start their own families in other sections of the refuge.

Partly because of Hope's efforts, we know a lot more today about beavers and their habits. Beavers build dams, which often cause flooding. In the wild, this helps animals. They cannot turn on a faucet when they want a drink. A beaver pond provides water to drink, minnows and plants to eat, and reed-covered places to hide. Many creatures are attracted to the wet, marshy habitat that beavers call home.

But sometimes beaver dams cause problems for people. When a dam floods a road, people get angry. They might think the answer is to get rid of the beavers. But there is a better solution. As the manager of Unexpected Wildlife Refuge, Hope shows people how to deal with beaver-related problems. "I try to show people that humans and beavers can live together in peace," she says.

For instance, Hope teaches others how to build a "beaver stop." This device lets water flow through a tunnel under a road—instead of flooding over the road. That helps keep drivers happy. Hope also recommends the use of a "beaver baffler." This structure keeps beavers from building dams near large drainpipes.

Beavers cut down trees to make their dams. Some people do not like having trees on their property cut down—even by beavers. Hope shows them how to protect their trees with a special kind of wire fencing. It is like saying to a beaver, "Please find another tree."

As the manager of Unexpected Wildlife Refuge, Hope works hard to show people that humans and beavers really can learn to live side by side. Today, beavers are no longer endangered in New Jersey—thanks, in part, to her efforts. Over the years, the refuge has grown in size from eighty-five acres to more than four hundred acres. It is now owned by a nonprofit organization that Hope started—the Beaver Defenders.

Managing the refuge is a big job. It means patrolling the land for beaver traps and removing them. It means posting "No Trespassing" signs. Hope also patrols the land to make sure no hunters stray into this protected area. Much of the work, like clearing brush or mending fences, is difficult and dirty. One of Hope's least favorite tasks as a private wildlife refuge manager is "the never-ending paperwork" connected with running a nonprofit organization.

Managing the refuge also involves organizing dozens of volunteers. They patrol the refuge to make sure animals stay safe. They put up birdhouses. They help maintain more than ten miles of trails. They even cut the grass at Bluebird Field, a two-acre meadow area that must be mowed at certain times to provide just the right habitat for its rare North American songbirds. On a few acres of the refuge, squash, pumpkins, corn and mixed grains are grown as food for the wildlife. Thanks to all this hard work, the refuge is home to many creatures—beavers and bluebirds as well as swallows, nuthatches, prothonotary warblers, wood ducks, herons, screech owls, deer, squirrels and chipmunks.

Because Hope works in a privately owned wildlife refuge, her work is a little different from that of many wildlife refuge managers. Most wildlife refuges are managed by people who work for federal and state agencies. These managers must sometimes focus on regulating animal populations, rather than on protecting individual animals. For example, when an animal population is too large, these managers often must encourage people to hunt within their refuges.

Many wildlife refuge managers have an undergraduate degree. Depending on the job, additional training or schooling may be required, such as a master's degree in environmental management or education. Refuge jobs with the federal government usually have stricter requirements.

Hope's work as the manager of a privately owned wildlife refuge gives us two important things to consider. First, a person who is truly dedicated to animals and the environment can make a life's work out of protecting wildlife and nature on their own land. Second, the need for wildlife refuges and parks to protect animals and their habitats will only grow with time. As Hope has shown us, the most important part of managing a refuge is having a love and respect for animals—and the desire to treat them humanely.

Could You Have a Career as a Wildlife Refuge Manager?

Do you have a strong commitment to protecting wildlife and the environment? Are you comfortable working outdoors in all kinds of weather? Would you like hands-on, outdoor tasks, like putting up birdhouses, filling feeders, mending fences and clearing brush? If so, a career as a wildlife refuge manager might be the thing for you. Here are some ideas for further exploration:

1. Learn more about the wild animals that live in your area. Practice using a field guide to identify birds and other creatures. Keep a list by your front door of all the wild animals you see in your backyard or town. Don't forget insects!

2. Using the list you made for the above activity, write down all the strategies you can think of for helping or protecting the wildlife that lives in your area. Share what you learn with others—maybe in a report to your class.

3. Talk to the manager of a nearby wildlife refuge. Find out about the rewards and frustrations of that person's career. If possible, volunteer to help out at that refuge or at a nearby nature center.

part five
Careers in the Arts

Look around your home, school library or classroom. How many pictures, poems and stories about animals can you find? Animals have inspired human creativity from as long ago as the days of the ancient cave paintings. Fascinating photographs, films, paintings, stories and music have all been inspired by animals. Bats, birds, insects, reptiles, mammals and more have served as the subjects of jewelry, statues, wood carvings, poems and even buildings for architecture. Photographers, filmmakers, writers, artists and musicians alike have been inspired by the beauty, character and spirit of animals.

Today our natural resources are shrinking rapidly. But some creative individuals are still finding ways to help us appreciate animals and the environment. There is a growing demand for those who can use their art to help others care about the feathered, furred and scaled beings with which we share Earth.

A Career in the Arts

Although there are many opportunities to focus on animals with a career in the arts, the competition in all artistic fields is fierce. The pay, especially when starting out, is often extremely low. To be successful, people need to be competitive as well as creative, and must have lots of practice and strong skills in their field of art. Many artistic professions require a person to travel.

Simply being good at art, writing, music or photography is not enough if you want to make a job of it. You will need good business skills as well. Professionals in the arts are often self-employed, which means they are responsible for advertising and selling their work, billing clients for their creative services and keeping track of their business expenses. Running your own business takes self-confidence, organization, discipline and hard work.

Preparing for a Career in the Arts

Photographers, filmmakers, writers, artists and musicians all need to have formal training in their craft. Instructional classes are important in developing any artistic skill. Classes in photography, filmmaking, writing, drawing, painting, sculpting and music are often available locally. There are also schools and colleges that specialize in each of these areas. Many people who want to pursue a career in writing and communications obtain a college degree in English or liberal arts. Many artists attend art school, while musicians may attend a conservatory.

Learning from the work of others is another form of education. Often you can gain a greater appreciation for the creative work of other artists through books, magazines, films, musical recordings and art exhibits, as well as through live performances such as poetry readings and concerts. Submitting work for competition (or simply attending art competitions) is another way to learn more about an art form. Perhaps the best way to learn, however, is to practice. This holds true for almost any art form. If you really want to pursue an animal-related career in writing or painting, for instance, you should try to write or paint every day.

The Work of the Animal Photographer

One way to develop your skills in animal photography is to take lots of photographs of animals. That alone, however, is not enough if you are interested in photography as a career. For one thing, you have to learn the technical skills of photography. A professional animal photograph is more than just a pretty picture. Rather than using words, it uses light and images to tell a story about the animal. It also meets good design characteristics, just like a painting or drawing.

Different animal photographers specialize in taking different kinds of photographs. Many photographers specialize in one category of animal—marine mammals, pets or endangered species, for instance. Today's market for animal photography is good. Professional photographs are used in books, magazines, television, video production, advertising, greeting cards and more.

Many photographers sell the rights to the use of their photographs through businesses called stock houses. A publisher contacts the stock house to obtain the right to use a certain photograph. The photographer then receives an amount of money based on how the photograph will be used and how many copies of the item in which the photograph is to appear will be produced. The stock house takes a portion of the money to pay for the service it provides to the photographer.

Working as a Video Producer

Like the photographer, the video producer may also make a living capturing animals on film—but by taking moving pictures rather than still ones. The kind of animals photographed depends on the kind of video being made. Many independent video producers create their programs for a specific client. For example, a state's department of environmental protection might want to improve the public's understanding of endangered species within the state. The department might hire an independent video producer to make a film, which might then be aired on local television channels. If the program is successful, larger television stations might air it as well. Or, the program might be sold to schools and shown to students in biology and environmental studies classes. Video television programming is an exciting format for reaching the public.

Training in video production often consists of taking classes offered locally and/or attending a college with a strong department in this area. Just watching video programs can also be helpful in developing some skills. Excellent photography skills, a willingness to travel, and good business skills are needed for this career as well.

Writing About Animals

For the writer who specializes in animal-related topics, there are many avenues to explore. You could become a fiction or nonfiction writer, a poet, a film or video scriptwriter, or a writer/editor for a national nonprofit animal protection organization like The Humane Society of the United States.

Most writers specialize in a particular kind of writing. This doesn't mean just writing the same way all the time. It means taking stock of your abilities and concentrating most of your effort on what you do best. If you are especially good at making up your own animal stories or poems, for instance, you might want to specialize in fiction. In that case, your goal would most likely be to have your work published in magazines or books. Nonfiction writers also seek to have their work published in magazines and books, as well as in newspapers. As a scriptwriter, your work might be aired on television in the form of a program about animals. And if you were to write for a nonprofit organization, your writing would typically focus on teaching people about animals.

A nature or animal story writer needs to read and write about animals as often as possible to develop writing skills and learn about his or her subject. "Where do you get your ideas?" is a question many experienced writers are often asked. Developing writing topics to write about is as important as having excellent writing skills. Although pencil and paper are tools of the trade, most writers use a computer and word-processing software to keep up with the demands of publishers and other business clients. Developing computer and word-processing skills is vital for any writer in today's business world.

Working as an Artist

The artist who draws and paints animals works in an extremely competitive field. Different jobs call for different artistic techniques. Being skilled at a range of drawing, painting and graphic-design techniques is important.

There are many avenues open to the person who wants a career creating original animal artwork. Professional wildlife artists might sell their paintings through art galleries. Some artists specialize in painting pet portraits. They might advertise their services through art galleries, veterinary hospitals, pet supply stores and humane societies. Working as a children's book illustrator is also a possibility. And there are other fields as well, such as greeting card art and graphic design. For some who are just starting out, an artistic career may be a weekend pursuit conducted while working full- or part-time at another animal-related job.

Animals and the Professional Musician

Nineteenth-century composer Claude Debussy, with his "Afternoon of a Faun," was not the first musician to be inspired by animals. Animals have found their way into countless folk songs and musical compositions over the years. Today, more musicians than ever before take their inspiration from animals. Many are even incorporating the grunts, squeaks and squawks of animals into their music.

Working as a professional musician often involves traveling, conducting music workshops and performing all across the country. Many musicians spend part of each year "on tour" giving performances and the rest of their time teaching music to students near their home or in major cities. This might sound exciting—and it is—but adapting to a performance schedule can be very challenging for the musician, not to mention the musician's family and pets.

Full-Time vs. Freelance Employment

A career in the arts that relates to animals can involve full-time or freelance work. If you are employed full-time, you can expect to earn a steady salary as well as receive benefits including paid vacations, sick leave and health insurance. Your work schedule will probably remain very constant. If you like working with others, you might prefer the formal, full-time work setting. On the other hand, what you gain in security you might lose in personal creativity, because you will be pursuing your artwork in a way and at a pace that suits your employer.

The alternative—working as a self-employed freelancer—is not right for everyone. Although the freelancer may have more creative freedom and more freedom in choosing his or her schedule, freelancing involves uncertainty, because the clients themselves often determine how much work you will receive. Your workload is almost sure to fluctuate, so you will need to adapt your work schedule to the amount of work available. Some days you will probably have too much work, and other days there may not be enough work to keep you busy. In addition, you will also have to pay for your own health insurance (a significant expense) and you will not get paid for sick time.

As a freelancer in the arts, you can probably also expect to work on your own, instead of in an office with other people. This suits some people, but others find that working by themselves makes them feel lonely. You will need to balance the satisfaction of exercising your creativity and choosing your own work schedule against how you feel overall about the independence and uncertainty of working freelance.

Choosing Your Career

Competition in the arts is very fierce. But if you are interested in pursuing an animal-related career in the arts, don't be hopelessly discouraged. Some people start out by working in an unrelated full-time job while keeping their art alive on a part-time or freelance basis. Working on holidays, weeknights and weekends may not be your idea of fun. But it is one way to establish yourself as a photographer, writer, painter, musician or other art professional. Even if you decide not to make a full-time, part-time or freelance career of your animal-related art, time spent developing your artistic abilities and appreciation is never time wasted. It will bring joy, discipline and self-confidence into your life every day.

chapter 22
PHOTOGRAPHER

Bob Talbot with a 35mm motion picture camera on Free Willy II *shoot.*

The morning mists were heavy when a commercial whale-watching vessel pulled out of a southern California marina. It was followed by a smaller motorboat. The passengers aboard this small boat included a fourteen-year-old boy and his friends, and all were anxious to see whales. Before long they were among a pod (a family) of gray whales. They watched eagerly for signs of movement. Suddenly, a few yards away, a whale surfaced. The huge creature blew a spray of water into the air. Then, raising an enormous tail high into the air, the whale gracefully slid beneath the surface of the water.

For a long time afterward, the boy would think about seeing his first whale. He wondered where the whale might be and what the animal's undersea world was like. The boy did not know that he, Bob Talbot, would one day become a famous marine mammal photographer. For now, it was enough to experience the magic and wonder of a life so different from his own.

Soon after high school, Bob began working as a commercial photographer. He had photographed his first whale on that misty day when he was fourteen. A teacher had encouraged his photography skills. As a young man, though, Bob never dreamed he could actually make a living photographing whales. He just knew he had to keep doing what he loved. One day the president of a publishing company saw one of Bob's whale photographs in a magazine and tracked him down. Before long, Bob's photos were appearing as posters printed by Mirage Editions. Today, Bob's Mirage images are sold all around the world and are one of the most popular poster series ever created.

For the past twenty years, Bob Talbot has given the world some of the finest photographs ever taken of whales, dolphins, seals and other marine mammals. As posters and prints, his photographs have sold in the millions worldwide. His work has appeared in many books and magazines. His wildlife footage has been seen on network television and in major motion pictures.

A successful animal photographer does more than take great pictures. Each photograph must say something unique about the magic and mystery of its animal subject. Animal photographers must be able to capture their passion and excitement about wildlife or pets in their photographs. "When I'm out on the ocean with dolphins or whales," says Bob, "I feel like saying, 'Oh, you gotta see this!'" That feeling of "you gotta see this!" is an important ingredient in every one of his photographs.

Photographing animals takes a lot of patience. A marine mammal photographer often takes pictures of his or her subjects from a boat. The animals and the boat are constantly moving. The light is always changing. The weather can be unpredictable too. Despite all these variables, the photographer must keep the camera steady and keep refocusing. In addition, wild animals can be shy. You cannot be sure what they will do. Photographing them at sea—or anywhere else—is a challenge.

Most people would be surprised to learn how much time it takes to capture a great image on film. For every hour spent actually photographing marine animals, Bob and his team spend about twenty hours making preparations, traveling and just plain waiting. It can take a long time—days or weeks. "Not quitting after the third week" is what makes Bob so successful, according to one of his assistants.

In addition to time, photographing animals in the wild can take a lot of money. The cost is even greater when a photographer works with a team of assistants, rather than alone. In Bob's case, his team members help set up equipment for the photo shoots, and also manage the boat and diving gear. A photographic expedition may cost many thousands of dollars.

Like many wildlife photographers, Bob only photographs animals in their natural habitats. He feels strongly that his work should not bother the animals. If he senses that the animals are disturbed by his presence, he leaves. How do you know when marine mammals would like you to go away? Over the years, Bob has come to understand the ways of the marine mammals he photographs. Sometimes they show their displeasure by changing their swimming pattern. Or they may change the amount of time they spend breathing between dives, or the length of their dives.

Through working as a photographer, Bob has come to appreciate and care deeply about the animals he photographs. "There's a group of dolphins we visit regularly in the Bahamas," he says. "We recognize them and we've seen their babies grow up. I think that's what a lot of people miss. They see these animals as just a bunch of 'fish.' It's not like that. These animals are very affectionate with each other. They have very close family groups. They play together and work together."

In addition to his work in still photography, Bob is also a filmmaker. His film footage has appeared in network television productions and in the major motion picture *Free Willy* and its sequel. Bob's scenes of whales in the wild showed how much Willy had lost by being captured and kept in an aquarium. It was a powerful statement.

Bob Talbot is concerned about the ocean as well as the animals who live there. He has captured on film the devastation caused by oil spills. For someone who cares about animals as much as Bob does, witnessing this devastation is difficult. But he wants to help people understand what happens to animals when an oil spill takes place—so that spills can be prevented in the future.

In a sense, an animal photographer is an educator. Through photographs, he or she teaches people to appreciate animals and their habitats. "What I try to do in my work," Bob says, "is to show animals in a way that will encourage people to care about them. I try to present animals as individuals. I think it is easier for people to have compassion for, say, an individual whale than for 'whales' as a group. By caring about an individual animal, people begin to develop compassion for the group as well." What a great way to fulfill an artistic dream and help animals at the same time!

Talbot's "La Petite Baleine" captures the beauty of mother and calf Humpback whales.

© BOB TALBOT

Photographer

Could You Have a Career as a Photographer?

Do you have patience and a love of animals? Are you a practical person who is willing to develop good business skills? If so, a career as an animal photographer might be right for you. Here are some ideas to explore:

1. Bob Talbot has some expert advice just for young people interested in a career in photography: "Take as many pictures as you can. Most of all, learn from every picture you take." Put together a portfolio of your best photographs. If possible, display your work at school or at a local library. Or, organize a wildlife photograph contest at your school.

2. Photo exhibitions, magazines, calendars and books of photographs can be great resources. Learn all you can about photography by studying the work of others. You can see Bob Talbot's photographs in calendars and notecards available nationwide, as well as at his website: http://www.talbotcollection.com/. Ask for his video *Dolphins & Orcas* at your public library.

3. If your school has a photography club, join it. If it doesn't, why not start one? For more information about nature photography, write to the North American Nature Photography Association, 10200 W. 44th Ave., #304, Wheat Ridge, CO 80033, or visit their website at http://nanpa.org/nanpa.htm.

chapter 23
VIDEO PRODUCER

Video producer and president of Environmental Media Corporation Bill Pendergraft strives to teach people about protecting animals and the environment.

© ENVIRONMENTAL MEDIA CORPORATION

The sleek, young black bear was munching fallen apples at the edge of the woods. Suddenly she raised her head. She sniffed the air uncertainly. Something was not right, but she was not sure what was bothering her. She had a feeling of being watched. Yet no people were in sight. She looked around. No, not a single human.

This is just what Bill Pendergraft, video producer and president of Environmental Media Corporation, had worked so hard to make her think. Filming from behind a blind—a natural screen set up to hide a filmmaker from animals—he captured some wonderful footage of the bear for use in the video he was producing.

Bill's company creates and sells educational videos about animals and the environment. Like many independent video producers, he covers different jobs in his work. He is a writer, editor, film director, photographer, manager and more. He encounters many kinds of animals on the job, from snakes to swans to sea turtles.

On any given day, an independent video producer may find him- or herself in the office editing a script, outdoors directing a production crew or in the studio editing film. Each job is interesting in its own way. The production of a film starts with a spark—an idea. Bill believes that allowing time for thinking and reflecting is important for everyone. "Having experiences and thinking about them gives you a set of tools for understanding the world," he says. "When people think about their experiences, that is when learning takes place."

The next step is to develop a script. This involves writing and editing. Effective communication takes time—especially when the message is so important. "People often don't understand how animals depend on one another and the environment—or how the environment depends on animals. These relationships are complex," says Bill. Like many video producers who specialize in environmental topics, he wants to help people better understand the issues and learn to protect animals and the earth.

One of Bill's recent projects was a film about jellyfish. Some people might not think of a jellyfish as an animal they would like to protect. Yet every species of animal is important. Bill was filming a kind of freshwater jellyfish that is in danger from humans. Tourists to the tropical islands of Palau where the jellyfish live often don't understand how important these animals are. By swimming in the lake with the jellyfish and sometimes catching them, tourists harm the animals. Bill hopes that his film will help change this.

Although each script is carefully crafted, most video producers do not follow their scripts exactly. Instead, the script provides a framework for shooting the film. As Bill explains, "When we shoot film, it is important to stay open to what goes on around us. We try to be good listeners and watchers. As we go along, we get more ideas for what to include."

The task of filming involves being outdoors and directing the production crew. Environmental Media Corporation produces videos for clients all around the world. A client may be an individual, a company, a nonprofit organization or a government agency. Bill's work has taken him to places as nearby as the Appalachian Mountains in his home state of North Carolina and as far away as a tropical island in the Pacific Ocean.

A lot of planning goes into shooting a film. Producing just a fifteen-minute program takes months of filming, sound recording and interviews. The people doing these jobs must be flexible about the hours they work. "We work directly with nature," says Bill. "So we have to adapt ourselves to that world. To photograph animals, we often must be on-site before the sun is up, or long after dark." While filming the life cycle of loggerhead sea turtles, for instance, Bill and his crew kept "turtle hours." They spent a moonlit evening filming a nest of more than one hundred babies as they hatched and streamed out into the sea. "It was incredible to watch," he says.

The film crew must be prepared to deal with different kinds of terrain, climate and weather. Bill has directed films in rain forests, in deserts, on beaches, on mountains and in underwater coral reefs. On a recent shoot in the Grand Canyon, for example, temperatures were in the fifties in the morning, yet had topped one hundred degrees by noon.

A day of editing in the studio is much different from a day of hiking in the desert. When the video producer is in the studio, he or she is more likely to work a nine-to-five schedule. Studio equipment is used to run the film footage. The producer decides which scenes to keep in the video and which scenes to cut. "We shoot much more film than will appear in the final product," Bill explains. "Deciding what to leave out is as important to the film as deciding what to leave in."

When the video is finished, the work is only partly done. It is not enough simply to create a film. The film must be advertised and sold so that others can experience it. Various staff members at Environmental Media Corporation are responsible for duplicating and distributing the programs. As president of the company, however, Bill must keep track of all the work that is done.

Video production is a team effort, so an ability to work well with others is an important on-the-job skill. "Video production is not a 'lone-wolf' job," says Bill. "A whole 'pack' of people are involved, including writers, editors, photographers, scientists, video producers, teachers and more."

Is there a downside to this exciting job? Perhaps. Some video producers who focus on environmental issues are concerned that much of their work is archival. This means they are making a record of animals and habitats that may not be around for much longer. For instance, a couple of years ago Bill worked with a plant scientist on a video about endangered pitcher plants. "We were shooting in a tiny spot in the woods in North Carolina. That little area of land could easily become a shopping mall in the next few years," he observes. "As the human population continues to grow and our use of resources is focused on making money, large areas of land that animals need in order to survive are being lost," he says. "Once a habitat is destroyed, it is usually gone for good."

Teaching people about the need to protect animals and their habitats is one solution to this problem. As a film producer and director, Bill uses his talents to teach people about wild animals and, hopefully, inspire them to think, learn and care.

Could You Have a Career as a Video Producer?

Do you like writing, filming, traveling and working with others? Would you be willing to spend hours in the hot sun or a frosty wind just to get great footage of a wild animal? If so, an animal-related career in video production might be right for you. Here are some suggestions for further exploration:

1. If you are interested in making films and videos as a career, start by watching animal-related programs on television and thinking about how the different scenes might have been filmed. Does the animal appear close up or far away? What role does lighting play in producing the images? Consider sound, action and script development. Think critically about each nature program you watch and discuss it with your family.

2. Ask your teacher if you can do a school project that involves viewing one or more nature videos. Bill Pendergraft's videos are available from Environmental Media, P.O. Box 1016, Chapel Hill, NC 27514; see their website at http://www.envmedia.com/. Your school media center may already have some of these videos. If not, ask your teacher to arrange for your school to receive copies.

3. Try writing your own script and shooting a video about wild animals that live in your area. You may be able to borrow or rent a video camera through your school. Or maybe someone in your family has one you can use. Share your video with family, friends and classmates.

4. Another good place to look for animal videos is on the Internet at www.animalchannel.net, a website produced by The Humane Society of the United States.

chapter 24
WRITER

Photographer and nature writer Hope Ryden spends many long hours in the wild observing the animals she writes about.

© HOPE RYDEN

Sunlight filtered gently through the leaves. The young girl followed a familiar path deeper into the forest. She knew this woodland area in northern Wisconsin well. She had spent many happy days here at her family's summer cabin. The snap of a twig caught her attention. Looking across a bush, she glimpsed a large, gray, furry body, a black nose … and a pair of green eyes watching her every move.

The girl had heard rumors that a lone wolf was in the area but had not thought much about it. Now, instead of fear, she felt only fascination for those intelligent eyes as they stared back into hers. What was the wolf thinking? Wolves had been nearly wiped out in Wisconsin. Why was this one wandering alone instead of with a pack? As if in answer to her unspoken questions, the great silvery creature turned away and loped off, moving easily through the trees. For a moment, the girl stood still with wonder. Then, eager to share her wild vision, she hurried back to the cabin and her family.

In time, the girl's fascination with animals and nature would lead her to an exciting career. Imagine leaving for your job at about the time of day when most people are returning from theirs! That is what Hope Ryden often does. Hope is a naturalist, photographer and author who observes and writes about wild animals. Many of those animals, like coyotes, beavers and bobcats, are active at night. So Hope often spends night after night, in all kinds of weather, observing animals and taking notes.

Hope has written many books for young people. Her ideas come from the natural world around her. One book, *The Raggedy Red Squirrel,* was inspired by a tree squirrel living in a birdhouse at her weekend cabin in upstate New York. *The ABC of Crawlers and Flyers* is about the fascinating world of insect life in her own backyard. Yet Hope's books have not always kept her close to home. Her work has taken her to the Florida Keys, the western United States and Australia, among other places.

Before writing a book, a writer typically submits his or her idea to a publisher. If the book idea is accepted, the writer can begin work. Then, a nonfiction book needs to be researched carefully. Hope conducts some of her research using books and other resources. Most of her research, however, comes from her own fieldwork—her observations of animals. To prepare for fieldwork, she visits the habitat where the animals live and selects a place from which to watch them.

Gathering material for a book is not a speedy process. It takes time and patience. Hope observed beavers near her home for four years in order to write *Lily Pond*, a book for adults, and *The Beaver*, a book for children. Much of her observations were made at night, when the beavers were active. "When the beavers came out, I watched and listened," says Hope. "In the summer months, the days are long. The beavers came out early enough that I had a few hours of daylight. Often I watched them until well after midnight. I would sit in the same place. I wanted to let them get used to me. I used binoculars to observe clearly what they were doing." Hope also took her own photographs to use in illustrating her books about the beavers.

Writer

A field guide is useful to many nature writers. It helps the writer identify exactly what kind of animal he or she is looking at. A journal for taking field notes is also a must. And a camera is an important tool for nature writers who, like Hope, want to illustrate their writing with photographs. Understanding the technical aspects of photography—how to take the perfect picture—is an important skill.

Appreciating each animal for its uniqueness is part of what makes Hope an excellent nature writer. She often gives her subjects special names, like the Raggedy Red Squirrel or the Inspector General—her nickname for the large beaver of *Lily Pond* who carefully inspected his dam each night for leaks.

The process of creating a book follows a kind of cycle, from idea to fieldwork to the recording of experiences in writing and photography, to the production of a final manuscript. Then the cycle begins again with a new idea. The nature writer's work demands constant patience, attention to detail and the spark of creativity.

It is no accident that many of Hope's books are about North American wildlife. Like many nature writers, she thinks that people here have not paid enough attention to the animals who live right in their own forests, ponds and streams. She thinks that people are often more interested in animals from other continents—animals like tigers, elephants and chimpanzees. Yet the lives of animals here are just as important, just as fascinating.

Like many writers who focus on animals and their habitats, Hope would like to interest more people in the wild animals around us. She believes that if people learn more about these animals, they will come to appreciate them. When people appreciate wild animals, they are less likely to capture or harm them. And perhaps they will be more likely to set aside land where animals can live in their natural habitats. That is something Hope would like to see happen.

She encourages her readers to be open to nature. "Even if you cannot stay outside late or travel to exotic places to watch wildlife, there is plenty to see," Hope reminds us. "The main thing is to find an animal that lives near you and see how much information you can discover about that animal for yourself—because discovery is the most fun of all!"

Could You Have a Career as a Writer?

Could observing and writing about animals be the job for you? Here are some ideas to help you decide:

1. Hope suggests observing a favorite pet as one way to get started observing and writing about animals. She and her husband have a dog who was adopted from an animal shelter and a cat who they took in as a stray. Hope's pets served as inspiration for her books *Your Cat's Wild Cousins and Your Dog's Wild Cousins*. Hope also recommends keeping a nature journal as a way to practice observation and writing about wild animals.

2. You can learn a lot about writing just by reading what others have written. One writer may use lots of descriptive words, while another may focus on plain action. Explore different writing styles. While you're at it, be sure to see these books by Hope Ryden: Nonfiction—*Your Cat's Wild Cousins, Your Dog's Wild Cousins, Joey: The Story of a Baby Kangaroo, Little Deer of the Florida Keys, Bobcat, America's Bald Eagles, The Beaver, ABC of Crawlers and Flyers,* and *Out of the Wild: The Story of Domesticated Animals;* and Fiction—*Backyard Rescue and Wild Horse Summer.*

3. If you have written any essays or stories about animals, share them. You might even enter them in local and national writing competitions. Budding, young writers should also visit these two websites: http://www.kidpub.org/kidpub/ and http://www.kids-space.org.

chapter 25
ARTIST

Wildlife artist Julie Zickefoose is best known for her paintings and drawings of birds.

The sky was blue and cloudless as a mother and her tiny daughter walked through the old orchard. Many years before, this land had been used for farming. Now only the gnarled, barren trees remained. The girl was the first to spot the bluebird perched on a branch. Quickly, her mother grabbed a pencil and paper from her pocket and made a hasty sketch. The little girl was not surprised. Ever since she could remember, seeing wild birds and watching her mother capture them in simple sketches had been part of her world. That's what it was like to be the daughter of Julie Zickefoose, a wildlife artist and naturalist.

Although she sometimes paints mammals and plants, Julie Zickefoose is best known for her paintings and drawings of birds, most of which she creates for books and magazines. Julie does her sketching outdoors. She does her watercolor paintings in a studio in her home—an old farmhouse in Ohio surrounded by meadows, forests and an orchard. The area provides an ideal place for observing many kinds of songbirds and other animals.

Julie's work is different from that of many of the professionals featured in this book in a special way: She works at home and combines her artistic career with being a full-time mother. "Working at home is not like getting up and going to an office every day," she explains. Julie needs to be especially disciplined about her work. She devotes part of every day to drawing or painting. Like most artists, when there is a deadline to meet she may work nonstop.

As the mother of a two-year-old, Julie's workdays are full of interruptions. Most of the time, however, her daughter Phoebe enjoys watching her work. "I do a lot of artwork for children's magazines like *Spider*, *Cricket* and *Ladybug*. My daughter Phoebe loves seeing my artwork in these children's publications," says Julie. "She also enjoys watching a picture grow." In addition to her work as an illustrator for magazines and books, Julie is a contributing editor to *Bird Watcher's Digest*.

Like many wildlife artists, Julie concentrates on two kinds of artwork—field sketches and paintings. A field sketch is done in pencil on sketch paper. It is drawn rapidly while directly observing an animal. After making a field sketch, a painting of the animal can be completed.

Julie paints in watercolors. She does her paintings from her own field sketches. By looking at photographs and reading about the animal she is painting, she is able to add details that she might not have captured in her sketch. She must research the animal—usually a bird—very carefully to be sure she portrays the details accurately.

"The real challenge with painting," says Julie, "is to give the image the same kind of life that the field sketch has. It is not the same as drawing with the animal alive and moving before your eyes." That "alive" quality is something all wildlife artists strive for in their work.

In addition to mastering drawing and painting techniques, a wildlife artist like Julie, who focuses on realism, needs to be very detail oriented. Julie tries to include as much information as she can in a painting without making her artwork look like a diagram. She puts all that she has learned about an animal into each drawing or painting. She tries to provide answers to questions like "What color is the inside of this bird's mouth?" "What food does this animal eat?" and "What habitat does it live in?" Julie takes pride in the accuracy of her paintings.

Any professional artist who creates art for magazines and books needs to pay strict attention to deadlines. An artist must have his or her artwork completed on time to meet the needs of the publishers who buy it. Like Julie, many artists sell one-time publication rights for their paintings and drawings to magazine and book publishers. This means a publisher is allowed to reproduce (photograph) the artwork one time and then must return it to the artist.

In addition to excellent technical skills, a freelance wildlife artist needs to have good business skills. The artist needs to fulfill the publisher's needs, meet deadlines, bill the publisher and keep track of payments and expenses. It is a big job, but a rewarding one.

Since she was a child, Julie has always been interested in nature and art. She graduated from Harvard University with a major in biological anthropology, but her real interest was drawing and painting birds. "I knew I wanted to continue learning about birds, watching them, drawing them, and developing the skills to become a good naturalist," she says. She started out by illustrating the thesis papers of other students. As she gained more experience, nature and art combined to become her full-time career. She spent six years working for the Nature Conservancy, where she designed endangered species preserves, observed and sketched birds, and worked to protect least terns and piping plovers. After that she turned her attention to freelance drawing and painting.

Much of Julie's work has an animal protection theme. She recently completed a painting of a Carolina parakeet. Because Carolina parakeets are now extinct, she had to study old paintings of the birds. "It made me sad as I worked on it to think that my daughter will never see one of these extinct birds," says Julie. "I hope my art might make people stop and think, 'Let's keep other kinds of birds from going the same way.'"

Seeing artwork can change a person's way of thinking, but it does not always have this effect. For that reason, Julie likes to help animals in a more direct way—by donating prints of her paintings to wildlife organizations. These organizations usually auction the prints to raise money for animal protection.

Just by looking at one of her paintings, you can see that Julie tries to capture the life spirit of her subjects. It is clear that she is serious about her work—deeply appreciating nature and the animals around her. That is what being a wildlife artist is all about!

© JULIE ZICKEFOOSE

"Crow's Play" by Julie Zickefoose. This talented artist helps animals by donating prints of her paintings to wildlife organizations.

Artist

Could You Have a Career as an Artist?

Do you have natural talent as an artist? Whether you like to draw, paint or model in clay, there is an artistic outlet available to you for expressing your feelings about animals. If you love animals and art, a career as a wildlife artist might be right for you. Here are some ideas for further exploration:

1. Get out into nature and practice drawing animals. Or draw your own pet. Draw the same animal again and again until you have captured it just the way you see it. Share your work with others and listen to their comments. Enter your paintings and drawings in local and national competitions. And check out this website as a place to share your animal art: http://www.kids-space.org.

2. Julie recommends a book for anyone interested in being an artist: *Drawing on the Right Side of the Brain* by Betty Edwards. Look for it at your public library. It is written for adults, but you and your parents may enjoy sharing it.

3. Study the art of professional wildlife artists. You can see Julie's artwork in the many books she has illustrated, including these two titles for young people: *Backyard Birds* (HarperCollins, 1993) and *Bird Watching for Dummies* (IDG Books, 1997). See Julie's artwork online at http://home.prizim.com/avesdel-sol/zickefoose.html.

4. You can find other examples of animal art all around you, from illustrated books to greeting cards to pet portraits. If you love art and animals, there are endless possibilities. Ron Burns is an artist who works closely with The Humane Society of the United States to bring attention to dogs and cats in shelters. You can see his pet portraits at www.ronburns.com.

chapter 26
MUSICIAN

Paul Winter has been combining the voices of animals with his music since the 1970s.

© LIVING MUSIC FOUNDATION

Take a walk in a park, the woods or your backyard. Stop for a moment and listen. Depending on the time, place and season, you might hear the buzz of a cricket, the chirp of a songbird or the scolding of a squirrel. Often, we overlook the language of animals. One person, however, has helped us hear the sounds wild animals make in a new way—as the music of nature. That person is Paul Winter.

Like many musicians, Paul plays with a group. The Paul Winter Consort was formed in 1967. The word "consort" dates from the period in history known as the Renaissance. Consorts were the house bands of the theaters in the time of Shakespeare. They were usually small musical groups in which each player had plenty of opportunity to improvise within the written parts of the music—much like the Paul Winter Consort does today.

In addition to Paul on his soprano saxophone, the Paul Winter Consort includes Paul Halley on piano and organ, Eugene Freisen on cello and Glen Velez on percussion instruments from around the world. In their music, the Consort partly relies on the technique of improvisation. Improvisation in music is when you play creatively without reading the sheet music or playing it from memory. The musicians of the Consort often improvise, or "grow" their music together, as they play.

Paul has been combining the voices of animals with his music since the 1970s. He was the first to do so; other musicians have since followed his lead. How did he get started? In 1968 Paul attended a lecture given by whale scientist Dr. Roger Payne. For many years, this famous wildlife biologist has made and studied underwater recordings of the sounds of whales.

Paul heard the songs of humpback whales for the first time at one of Dr. Payne's lectures. He was astonished by the beauty of the whales' voices. He was also fascinated by how complicated they were. He has described the whale songs he heard that day as having "as much variation as a Beethoven symphony." He later said about that experience, "It opened the doors of nature for me." As a result, Paul spent a good deal of time during the 1970s doing two things: He explored wilderness areas and he explored what the sounds of animals meant to him as a musician.

Ten years would pass before Paul would release his first album combining animal calls with his own music. *Common Ground* was released in 1977. On this album, listeners can hear the sounds of whales, wolves and eagles. Paul shared the money he made from the album with organizations that work to protect these animals.

Paul's music has been given different names. Some people call it jazz. Others refer to it as New Age music. Paul prefers to call it "Earth Music." He says this reminds him that his purpose is "to honor the earth and the whole tapestry of living beings of which I am a part."

Over the years, the Paul Winter Consort has recorded a variety of albums celebrating the earth and its animals. The album *Callings* brings together Paul's soulful music and the sounds of twelve sea animals. It re-creates a musical journey inspired by a sea lion pup who came ashore during one of Paul's whale-watching trips in the 1970s. *Canyon* is a celebration of the Grand Canyon recorded during a rafting trip. In

Whales Alive Paul combines his music, whale songs and whale poetry read by *Star Trek* actor Leonard Nimoy. *Earth: Voices of a Planet* is a musical tribute to the twentieth anniversary of Earth Day (in 1990) and features musical compositions honoring the oceans and the seven continents. *Prayer for the Wild Things* features the sounds of the Northern Rockies and won a Grammy Award for Best New Age Album in 1994.

One of Paul's most famous musical pieces is "Wolf Eyes," featured on an album by the same name. This work combines the haunting sound of Paul's saxophone with the wail of a timber wolf. It has become a Paul Winter Consort classic. When Paul plays it during a concert, he always ends with an invitation to his listeners. They are asked to participate by howling like wolves themselves. Paul believes that it is important for people, as well as a wolf pack, to give voice together. Howling is a good way to do this because there's no chance of a wrong note!

As a musician, Paul has traveled around the world. He has taken the special sounds of his vision of nature to concert halls in North and South America, Europe and Asia. He has also visited such places as the Grand Canyon, the Northern Rockies and Siberia's Lake Baikal to record the songs of animals for use in his music.

Working as a professional musician often involves traveling. Like Paul, many musicians spend part of the year giving concerts or conducting music workshops all around the country. Traveling can be very exciting. It can also be exhausting. Keeping up with a heavy performance schedule is demanding. It can be a strain on family, friends and pets. When a musician is not regularly performing, he or she may give private music lessons to students. Teaching students at home or through a local music school is another way in which musicians often support themselves.

To date, the Paul Winter Consort has won two Grammy Awards and seven Grammy nominations. Paul's music has helped bring attention to the plight of endangered species. It has awakened many people to the beauty of animals and their language. Paul has also given many benefit concerts to raise money for organizations that protect animals. He has successfully combined his appreciation for all life with an outstanding career as a musician.

Could You Have a Career as a **Musician?**

Do you have a favorite instrument? Would you like to use music to help people appreciate animals? If so, a career combining music with the language of animals might be right for you. Here are some ideas for further exploration:

1. If you want to make your living as a musician, the most important thing is to keep playing. As you play, think about your connection to animals and others. Paul has this to say about it: "Playing music and being outdoors are the two greatest things that any person can do, young or old. Music-making will awaken your mind, your body and your spirit. Through making music you will discover that you have a totally unique voice, be it your own voice or on your instrument. Music-making will bring you into community with your fellow musicians and with the people who listen to you. It will give you the opportunity to discover that you are connected to the great family of life on Earth—to the other ten million species of creatures as well as to people of different cultures."

2. Listen to music every chance you get. Be sure to listen to the music of the Paul Winter Consort, including these albums: *Callings, Canyon, Whales Alive!, Earth: Voices of a Planet, Prayer for the Wild Things* and *Wolf Eyes: A Retrospective*. Check for Paul's music at your public library, and to visit his website at http://www.livingmusic.com/.

3. To learn more about having a career as a musician, talk to a local music teacher or someone in your community who plays music professionally.

part six
Specialty Careers

The people who perform some animal-related jobs hardly ever see an animal. How can this be? Ask the landscaper who designs people's yards to make them wildlife-friendly. Ask the administrative assistant who keeps the office of a busy animal protection organization running smoothly. Ask the investment banker who manages portfolios for a humane society or an environmental protection organization.

People once thought of animal-related careers as being limited to the work that takes place in veterinary hospitals and animal shelters. That is no longer the case. Today, animal-related careers can be found far and wide. Almost anything that you can do professionally can be used to help animals in some way. You may never have thought about how some jobs could have an animal focus. Yet, with a slight twist, many occupations can indeed become humane careers.

Humane Careers with a Twist

Let's look at some examples. If you are good at sports, you might want to become a professional football player. How does playing football help animals? It doesn't, really. But if you were a famous sports figure, you might do commercials or public service announcements for a humane society or animal protection organization. Being a celebrity helps attract attention. People would notice you and listen to your message.

Let's say that your dream is to become involved in politics. Yet you would also like to help animals. Do you have to give up one of your goals? Not at all. You could run for public office and help pass laws to protect animals. Or you might become a lobbyist on Capitol Hill for a national organization that protects animals. Your job would be to explain to politicians why protecting animals is good for the politicians' constituents—the people who vote for them. Your efforts could translate into the passing of animal protection laws that might actually save the lives of millions of animals.

What about lawyers? You might not expect that some lawyers work closely with animal issues. Yet there are lawyers whose work benefits animals in many different ways. Some lawyers represent pets and their owners at trials. Others work at humane organizations to ensure that the work of these institutions runs smoothly and according to policy. A humane lawyer may give advice to people who want to pass animal protection laws. In almost any legal field, a lawyer can also help animals just by speaking to groups of other lawyers about the need for sensitivity to humane issues in the practice of law.

How about a job in office management? Do you have what it takes to be a leader? Are you responsible and organized? Are you good at directing the efforts of others and establishing priorities? If so, you may already have thought of one day putting your management skills to work to help animals. You could work in a variety of office settings at a variety of agencies—animal shelters, humane societies and animal protection organizations. Yet a good manager can work to help animals in other ways too—by running a publishing house that specializes in books or magazines about animals, for instance. The background for such career calls for a college education, management experience, and skills in writing and public speaking.

Perhaps your talents lie in working with your hands. You might create wildlife-friendly yards and gardens like those of the landscape designer featured in Chapter 29. Or you might develop your skills as a carpenter and help build animal enclosures for a wildlife rehabilitation center. You might even start your own business making and selling unusual bird feeders. With each bird feeder, you could enclose an educational message about protecting birds. That way you could help animals in two ways at once!

Humane Careers of the Future

As more people become interested in animals and develop compassion for their experiences, more animal-related careers are sure to emerge. Creative people who care about animals will help make a host of new animal-related jobs become reality. For some professions, adding an animal-related twist may become the key to having a successful business.

Perhaps you are good at managing money. You might become a financial manager—with a twist. Today, nonprofit organizations are able to keep operating partly because they receive donations from their members, and partly because they invest their money wisely. Many animal protection groups and environmental organizations invest a portion of their money to ensure future growth. These organizations often have concerns about just how their money is invested. For instance, a humane organization would not want to invest in biomedical companies that perform tests on animals. An environmental group would not want to support cutting down forests to build housing developments—even if it were a good investment from a moneymaking standpoint. A financial manager for a humane organization must be aware of such ethical considerations when investing the organization's money. It's an important job. A solid financial base ensures that nonprofit organizations can continue their valuable work to help animals and the earth.

What about a career in medicine? Studies show that caring for a pet can be good for people's health. Depending on what area of medicine you were to practice, your work might involve having your patients care for a pet as a kind of therapy. That would be good for the pet and good for the person as well.

With a degree in psychology or social work, combined with courses in animal behavior, you might start your own human/animal counseling service. Animals, like their human owners, have mental health–related problems. In fact, pet problems are increasingly being treated by veterinarians and trainers who specialize in animal psychology. Imagine it! People and pets working out their problems together, with you there to guide them.

Perhaps you have thought of becoming an architect and designing one-of-a-kind houses. What if your business were to have a unique twist? Your beautiful homes might feature a pet-friendly environment. For instance, you could design an area in a client's house to meet his or her cat's special needs—to climb, to play, to scratch, to feel sheltered. Or you could design homes with outdoor play areas for dogs. The possibilities are endless.

Sound farfetched? Jobs like these may become the wave of the future as more and more people come to value the animals with which we share our world.

Education for Specialty Humane Careers

Some specialty humane careers will always demand lots of education. A lawyer, for instance, must obtain an undergraduate degree, graduate from law school (an additional four years) and pass the bar exam for his or her state. Today, more law schools than ever before are offering courses in animal and environmental law. You can learn more by writing to various law schools and universities.

A classroom teacher who brings a humane focus to his or her work still needs to meet the same state educational requirements that other classroom teachers do. In most states, that means four years of college and two years of postgraduate work to get a master's degree in education. Special classes as well as certification may also be required.

In addition to teaching curriculum subjects, many teachers believe it important to help students develop values of kindness toward one another. A focus on humane education may mean taking extra courses and doing additional research. Although formal training in humane education is not a requirement for teachers, it can provide skills for helping students to develop into kinder, more compassionate adults. Self-training in this area usually comes from reading materials developed by humane organizations and, in some cases, educational organizations.

Some animal-related specialty careers can involve less formal education and more on-the-job training. The landscaper who designs wildlife-friendly gardens, for instance, might have a college degree in botany or biology. Or, he or she might learn to unite plants and animals by working as an assistant to a professional landscape designer or master gardener who specializes in this trade. Additionally, such a landscaper might have some background in art.

Using the Internet

If you have access to the Internet, learn all you can online about humane careers and the people who pursue them. Visit the websites of humane organizations, as well as websites of colleges and universities you may be interested in attending. More and more schools are offering courses related to animals—both pets and wildlife.

Choosing Your Career

Regardless of whether you want to be a lawyer, a lobbyist, a landscape designer, a teacher, an office manager or something else, adding an animal-related focus to your work will often mean more, not less, effort. But the benefits of knowing you have helped animals can be enormously rewarding.

More people are interested in animals today than ever before. As people become more aware of the animals around them, new and different animal-related careers will develop. There has never been a better time to combine work and a love of animals into an exciting career.

chapter 27
LAWYER

Lawyer Scott Beckstead protects the interests of pets and their owners through litigation.

For days, the large dog had sat chained to a tree. Biff was a lively husky-shepherd mix and craved exercise and attention. He eagerly wagged his tail whenever someone went by. Once in a while, a neighbor came into the yard and petted him. But most people were busy and did not bother to stop. "It's a shame the way that dog is treated," said one woman to her friend. "Such a beautiful dog too."

Fortunately, Biff had at least one friend. A young woman sometimes came into the yard and petted him. He was so excited by her attention that he would grab at her when she tried to leave. A couple of times, he had caught the hem of her dress in his teeth. But there was no harm done, so she continued to stop by and pet Biff whenever she saw him.

One day when the young woman stopped petting Biff and tried to leave, he grabbed at her and accidentally bit her wrist. The bite was serious enough that she had to go to a hospital emergency room. According to the law, she also had to inform the local animal shelter about what had happened. The shelter sent someone to pick up Biff. When Biff's owner learned of this, he said he wanted Biff to be euthanized. He did not want his dog anymore. That is when Scott Beckstead got involved.

Scott is a lawyer with a humane focus. He spends much of his day helping people resolve their legal problems. Many of these problems involve animals. "Let me tell you about Biff, one of my star clients," he says.

When the woman who had been bitten learned that Biff's owner wanted him to be euthanized, she contacted Scott. "She knew Biff had not bitten her to be mean," Scott explains. "It was an accident. The first thing I did was research the case. This meant spending some time with Biff. Next, I contacted Biff's owner. He agreed to sign a legal paper that I drew up. The paper said that the owner would no longer be responsible for Biff, and it gave ownership of Biff to me. I already had pets of my own and did not plan to keep Biff myself. But I needed to take ownership temporarily to protect him."

As Biff's legal owner, the first thing Scott did was to withdraw the euthanasia request. "Next," he says, "I contacted an expert in dog behavior." This woman spent time with Biff and got to know his habits.

"Next, we went to a hearing at dog court," says Scott. Where Scott lives, cases that involve dogs have their own court and judge. The expert testified before the dog judge. She said that Biff just needed some basic training. The judge listened to all the evidence and made a ruling.

"The ruling said that we would have to get training for Biff and find a good, permanent home for him," explains Scott. "And that is exactly what we did. Biff went to dog obedience school. Today he has a wonderful home with a big backyard to play in and a family who loves him. He is actually being trained to be a therapy dog. He will go to hospitals and nursing homes with his new owners to help cheer up the people there." All thanks to his lawyer.

Biff was one lucky canine client. Scott is pleased that, during the dog's trial, someone said Biff got better representation than many human clients. "I was thrilled to be involved in a case like Biff's," says Scott, "because I was so moved by the injustice of it."

A lawyer who wants to help animals can do what Scott does—protect animals from cruelty or injustice. A humane lawyer represents people who care about the interests of animals. Many of these cases involve pets, who are usually regarded as property. They have some legal protection under the law—such as the right not to be neglected or treated cruelly. Sometimes, however, protecting an animal means protecting the rights of the person who owns the animal. A humane lawyer protects people's legal interests to make sure their animals get the protection they need.

A humane lawyer can also help animals in another way—by becoming involved in politics and legislation at the city, state and national levels. Scott does this as well. "I use my skills as a lawyer to help make sure that laws protecting animals are written in a way that is legal, that makes sense and can be enforced," he says. "I spend time in the state capital talking to senators and legislators. I encourage them to pass laws that will help animals or not pass laws that will hurt animals." Does Scott have any political ambitions of his own? "I wouldn't rule anything out," he says with a smile.

Everyone knows that law school is challenging. Is there something Scott wishes he had known before he started down the path to becoming a lawyer? "I loved law school," says Scott, "because it taught me to think and figure out problems, but it came as kind of a shock to learn how much studying was required." He admits he wishes he had been more disciplined about studying before he got to college and law school. "Sometimes you don't see the point of what you are studying in school, but even if all you are doing is practicing your study skills, it is valuable," he says.

Scott loves his work. "Being a lawyer puts me in a position to really stick up for people and animals who need help," he says. It is not always easy. "Lots of times the people I deal with are upset. They may be angry. They may not want to listen to what I have to say. I've learned how to handle angry people, but it is not my favorite part of the job.

"What I like best, though," says Scott, "is that the law provides a way to empower people who care about animals. I like to think that my job is to step in and prevent others from hurting animals unnecessarily. I like that I have the ability to fight that fight—to change the minds of important people like judges and legislators—to get them started thinking in ways that mean they will do more to protect animals." Scott has turned his talents in reading, writing and speaking into a law career that helps both people and animals.

Could You Have a Career as a Lawyer?

Are you good at reading, writing and research? Do you enjoy talking to people? Do you want to help animals? If so, a career as a humane lawyer might be right for you. Here are some ideas for further exploration:

1. Improve your research and writing skills. Ask your teacher if you can do a special project about animal laws in your community. Start by contacting your local animal control facility or law enforcement agency.

2. Find out more about animal law by contacting the Animal Legal Defense Fund, 1363 Lincoln Ave., San Rafael, CA 90401, or by visiting their website at http://www.aldf.org/about.htm.

3. More and more law schools are offering courses in animal law. Find out all you can about a career as a humane lawyer by talking to a local lawyer who takes animal-related cases. Then, at your public library, research the names and addresses of one or more law schools. Write to them and ask whether they offer courses in animal law.

chapter 28
LOBBYIST

Lobbyist for The Humane Society of the United States, Ann Church represents the interests of animals in her work with legislators.

The vote was in progress. State legislators were deciding whether to allow the selling license platesto be sold with the words "Animal Friendly" on them. The money raised by the license plates would go to spaying and neutering programs. Lobbyist Ann Church held her breath. She had been working hard to encourage legislators to pass this law. How would the vote turn out? It passed!

"Whenever I see one of these license plates, it makes me feel good," says Ann. "Now there will be fewer unwanted pets, and more homes to go around for the pets who are already here—partly because of the work I did." Ann is a lobbyist for The Humane Society of the United States (HSUS), based in Washington, D.C. Her job is to help ensure that animal protection laws get passed.

Many of the laws being made around the country affect animals. Some are made in Washington, D.C., some in the state capitals and others in your own city or town. Laws passed at the federal level affect animals all around the country. Laws passed at the state level affect animals within a particular state. Laws passed at the local level affect animals within a particular county, city or town.

Are all these laws really necessary? "Absolutely," says Ann. "In order to protect animals, society *has* to make laws, because not everyone understands or cares about animals. Today every state has anti-cruelty laws. We work for laws that have to do with spaying and neutering animals, making sure that people license their pets, making sure that pets have rabies shots to protect people and animals, and protecting animals from neglect and cruelty," says Ann.

Laws are passed by people who work in government. The lobbyist works with government officials, and typically works for an organization, business or company. Lobbyists talk to lawmakers about the interests of their employer. Ann's employer, The HSUS, works to protect animals. Ann herself also cares deeply about animals, and she represents that interest when she works with legislators.

The lobbyist works with people at different levels of government. "Most of my day is spent talking with animal activists," says Ann, "and providing them with information. When someone gets a good law passed in one state, I take the information and the ideas they used to persuade lawmakers about the importance of their law. Then I share that information with people in other states who are trying to do the same thing. I see myself as someone who helps to spread information."

Sometimes the lobbyist works directly with legislators. "I call them and ask them to sponsor a bill that we believe will help animals," Ann explains. "That means they will get the bill going in Congress. Or I ask them to support a bill that is already in session—that is, being considered by Congress."

The lobbyist reviews many bills that are up for vote. He or she makes suggestions on how to change the language of a bill to make it stronger—so that it better protects animals. "How you say something in the law really matters," explains Ann.

"For example, you might have a law that says there should be no cruelty to animals. Only, the proposed law might define the word 'animal' as meaning only 'cats and dogs.' We believe people should not be cruel to any animal. So we might recommend changing the language of such a proposed law so that all animals will be protected under it."

Most lobbyists spend plenty of time writing. "When you work with legislation," Ann explains, "you are surrounded by so much information! So you need to express yourself in a way that gets right to the point." Most lobbyists have an undergraduate degree—often in political science, history or English. To increase a person's chances of employment in this popular field, a graduate degree—a master's or a doctorate—is also helpful. Legislative experience at the local, state or national level is often required.

After graduating from college, Ann got her legislative experience working for a U.S. senator. "Working for Senator Birch Bayh was thrilling," says Ann. "It is one thing to read about how our country's laws are passed. It is much more powerful to see that happen in person. While working for Senator Bayh, I came to really understand how laws are made. Senator Bayh was interested in many kinds of laws—including laws that protect animals. I was glad to find that I could do something I was good at and still help animals at the same time."

It is exciting to work for a U.S. senator, but what do you do if the senator is not reelected? Ann found out. "I met people from The HSUS through my work for Senator Bayh. When he was defeated in an election, The HSUS called the next day and asked if I wanted a job. I really enjoyed my work at The U.S. Senate. It taught me so much about lawmaking. But I am glad to be working for The HSUS. I feel that I can do much more to help animals here."

Ann is especially interested in helping to make anti-cruelty laws stronger. "Sometimes people think animal cruelty just has to do with animals. But it has a lot to do with people too. Studies show that when people hurt animals they often go on to hurt people too. Anti-cruelty laws make it possible to identify those people. That way, we can get help for them before they do serious harm to others and themselves."

Ann has combined her political interests and her love of animals into a successful career. "I've always been drawn to the legislative process," she says. "I am happy that I have found a way to put these two things together—legislation and helping animals."

Could You Have a Career as a
Lobbyist?

Do you like writing and public speaking as well as animals? If so, a career as a humane lobbyist might be right for you. Here are some suggestions to help you decide for yourself:

1. Become a class officer or get involved in your school government. Participating in a service club can also help you better understand how groups make decisions and take action to solve problems.

2. Learn more about how laws are passed where you live. If you don't know who your legislators are, start by finding out. You can get that information by calling your local library, League of Women Voters or Board of Elections. Call the toll-free telephone number for your state government, find out when the state legislation is in session and then arrange a visit. You can watch hearings and debates, and maybe even a voting session. Call ahead and find out if you can meet with your state legislator and if a tour of the state capitol can be arranged.

3. Go online to investigate legislation. Check out these federal government websites: http://www.whitehouse.gov/wh/welcome.html, http://www.senate.gov/ and http://www.house.gov. In addition, nearly all state governments have their own websites. Explore them as well.

4. Develop your lobbying skills! Legislators know that today's children are tomorrow's voters. Stay informed about animal laws being passed in your state and let your legislators know what you think. A handwritten letter is usually best.

chapter 29
HUMANE LANDSCAPE DESIGNER

Christine Cook designs gardens that delight people, while providing food and shelter for birds, butterflies and other creatures.

© CHRISTINE COOK

Imagine working in an office carpeted with soft, green moss. Instead of computers and file cabinets, your office furniture might consist of hollow logs and granite boulders. How would you like to have rabbits and chipmunks as your co-workers? When Christine Cook arrives at her workplace, she hears the flutelike song of the robin

Careers *with* Animals

instead of the hum of the photocopy machine. Christine is a humane landscape designer who manages her own business, called Mossaics.

Land is all around us. It's still there even when we cover it up with asphalt or concrete. Do people take the land for granted? Often the answer is yes. But not Christine.

People hire a humane landscape designer for different reasons. "Some people want plantings that provide food and shelter for all kinds of wild animals," says Christine. "They like the idea of sharing their yards with birds, butterflies, chipmunks, rabbits and other creatures." Others want to discourage a particular animal from coming to their homes. "For instance, some people want to discourage deer," explains Christine. "These people hire me to take out the plants and shrubs they already have that attract deer and replace them with plants that deer do not like to eat. This is a humane way to ask the deer to go someplace else."

Of course, Christine is also contacted by people who just want their yard to look like their neighbor's yard. "If I landscaped the neighbor's yard," she says, "that's fine. If someone else did the work, however, taking on the job can be a challenge." The yard may be full of invasive plants. Invasive plants actually kill off other, native plants. Christine may need to explain to a client that the beautiful burning bush in his yard is taking over the Northeast. "I would want to replace such a shrub with an American Cranberry Viburnum or other plant that is native to the area where I work—one that provides food and shelter for the wild animals who live here," explains Christine.

Can you guess how most landscape designers begin each day? By listening to the weather. "The weather is one thing that ties us all together—humans and animals alike," says Christine. "Finding out what the weather will be is crucial to my job because it determines whether I will be planting outdoors, or doing indoor work like designing, visiting nurseries and talking to clients."

Sometimes a school or nature center will hire a landscape designer to create a special garden—a butterfly garden, for instance. How does the landscape designer go about such an assignment? The first step is to visit the site. The landscape designer makes notes about what kinds of trees are nearby, how they might affect the garden, how much sun is available and what plants are already there. He or she also discusses with the clients how much money they want to spend, as well as their specific needs. Then, based on this information and the landscape designer's knowledge of native plants, he or she creates a design—in this case, a design incorporating plants that attract native butterflies.

The landscape designer often spends hours drawing and planning the best way to arrange the garden. He or she may need to research various plants. It is important that the landscape designer know exactly which flowers need certain insects for pollination and exactly which insects need certain flowers for food.

Designing a garden takes careful, detailed work. It is a little like painting a picture with flowers and shrubs. "I'm not just making a pretty picture, however," says Christine. "I have to focus on what plants like to grow together. I have to ask myself, 'What shelter will this design give wildlife? What birds will eat the berries of the shrub that I set out? What creatures will come to this dinner party that I am planning?'"

When the design is ready, the landscape designer shares it with the clients and makes changes based on their suggestions. Next, he or she must order plants from a nursery. "I may have to order different plants from different nurseries depending on who specializes in what," says Christine. "I also have to prepare the garden bed. This can take some time. The soil must be just right for certain kinds of plants. Finally, on a day when the weather is good, I gather the plants, take them to the site and plant them. You might think that planting the garden would take the most time, but it actually goes pretty quickly. What takes time is the researching, planning and design that go into the finished product."

Christine is concerned about the increase in land development around her. Often, the effects of land development on wildlife are not even a consideration. "I watch as developers cut down more and more trees. This bothers me because I know that those trees provide homes and food for animals. It is important to me to do what I can to replace shelter and food for animals wherever possible."

Does Christine have a green thumb? People often think of success with plants as if it were some kind of magic. "Actually," she says, "gardening success has more to do with meeting the needs of each plant. Different plants live in different habitats in the wild. Many rely on native wild animals for pollination and to spread their seeds. Some need a certain amount of water, shade or sun. Too much or too little doesn't work. The better we re-create the real-life habitat for each plant, the more success we are likely to have with it.

"What I like best about my work," says Christine, "is feeling I'm part of nature. I try to understand how everything works together. The more I learn about nature, the more I learn about myself and my place in the world." The environment could use more partners like this dedicated landscape designer.

© CHRISTINE COOK

A monarch butterfly enjoys the nectar of a native milkweed plant that Christine incorporated into one of her landscapes.

Could You Have a Career as a Humane Landscape Designer?

Do you love the outdoors and working with your head as well as with your hands? Do you want to help animals and the environment? If so, a career as a humane landscape designer might be right for you. Here are some ideas to help you decide for yourself:

1. Read about using gardening to attract birds, butterflies and other wildlife. Check out these books: *Growing Wild: Inviting Wildlife into Your Yard* by Constance Perenyi (Hillsboro, OR: Beyond Words, 1991) and *Worm's Eye View: Make Your Own Wildlife Refuge* by Kipchak Johnson (Brookfield, CT: Millbrook Press, 1991). While you're at it, check out these websites: http://www.monarchwatch.org/ (for information about butterfly gardening), http://www.fws.gov/r9mbmo/pamphlet/attract.html (for information about attracting wild birds) and http://www.edc.org/int/eepp/birds.html (for information about the Earth Education Partnership, a group of teachers and students working to solve environmental problems).

2. "Wildscape" part of your backyard or school yard (be sure to get permission first). Try planting shrubs and flowers that attract butterflies, hummingbirds and songbirds. Or create an area of tall grass or brush where animals can hide. Get more information at your local nature center.

chapter 30
CLASSROOM TEACHER

Teacher Carol Tracy helps students Kerri Devine, Andrew Lowe, and Anthony Siena learn more about earthworms.

© CAROL TRACY

Imagine you are in a fourth-grade classroom. Thirty students are seated at their desks. The teacher is writing something on the blackboard. Slowly, at the front of the room, a large, gray spider carefully lowers herself from the ceiling on a silken thread. Thirty pairs of eyes watch as the eight-legged creature lands lightly on the floor and begins crawling toward the class.

"That might be the beginning of chaos in some classrooms," laughs fourth-grade teacher Carol Tracy. "But not in mine." Carol teaches at Center School in East Hampton, Connecticut. Her students aren't bugged by bugs. They know exactly what to do. Thirty hands shoot into the air: "Mrs. Tracy, can I take the spider outside?" asks one student. "Can I?" asks another. "No, can I?" asks a third. "No, me this time. You did it last time," charges a fourth.

"Thank you," says Carol. "But I'll take her out myself." With that, Carol reaches for a plastic cup set aside for just this purpose. She puts the cup over the spider and slides a piece of cardboard under the cup's opening against the floor, trapping the little creature inside. Once outside, Carol quickly releases the spider without touching her.

"As a teacher," Carol explains, "I feel it is important to demonstrate to students that we share this planet. We don't own it." Showing kindness, even to spiders, is one way Carol teaches students about sharing Earth.

"One of the great things about teaching," Carol explains, "is that you never stop learning. Often, students think they are the only ones doing the studying. They don't realize that their teachers are always reading, always seeking out resources for information, always talking with experts on various subjects. Teachers need to do this so they can have the information to develop their classroom lessons." In Carol's case, this often means learning about animals and the environment. She tries to bring these topics into her classwork whenever possible.

As a student, you may think you have a pretty good idea of how a teacher's day begins. The teacher shows up in the classroom and starts teaching—right? Well, not quite. Most teachers must arrive at their classrooms very early in the morning—long before any students.

"I spend that extra time in several ways," says Carol. "I correct papers, write notes to students or parents, or coordinate sharing classroom materials with other teachers. I also think about any student who might need some extra attention that day. Maybe someone didn't do well on math the day before, or maybe they forgot their homework and got a white slip for it. It is my job to help that student understand that, even though he or she goofed the day before, it is okay to make a mistake and you have to get back on track."

Students arrive. First is the routine of taking attendance and making announcements. Then the class gets down to work. As a teacher teaches, he or she must stay aware of how long the lessons are taking. "The time goes by so fast," says Carol. "I have to fit everything in as far as what is being taught that day—and make it interesting as well." As a teacher with a humane focus, Carol might liven up her math lesson by tying it into a science lesson on bats. Or, for writing practice, she might have students write letters to the editor of the local newspaper about protecting a local wetland.

In science, Carol is required to teach a unit on food chains. "For this, I focus on earthworms," she explains. "I choose earthworms because kids' first reaction to these creatures is 'yuck!' Students start this unit thinking that earthworms are ugly and slimy. By the end, most of them are as in awe of these fascinating creatures as I am. They learn how earthworms improve the soil, move, and provide food for other animals."

Think your lunch break is never long enough? A teacher's lunch break is even shorter. "I eat lunch quickly while my students are at recess," says Carol. "Then I run down and stay with my students during their lunch break." Then it's back to more classwork.

"At the end of the day," says Carol, "I lead students through a process of review. We go over what we learned during the day and what homework needs to be done to be sure everyone understands what they need to do in order to start the next day." Then Carol takes students to their lockers and monitors them as they leave. "Different students are dismissed to different places," she explains. "Some go to after-school activities, some to daycare, some to buses, and others to cars or bicycles or to walk home. As a teacher, I have to be sure each student gets where he or she is supposed to be."

After students go home, the teacher goes home too. Right? Wrong. Afterschool time is important for teachers. "I use this time to touch base with my principal if there is a problem with a student," explains Carol. "I hold parent-teacher conferences, meet with older students, correct papers, clean the blackboard, put up new posters or bulletin boards and water the plants. Then I prepare for the next day of class." Carol never leaves her classroom without making sure that everything for the next day is in place. "I go through my units of study, plan how to begin teaching them, and lay out materials so that I won't be scrambling to find something the next morning.

"I remind my students that just because they are kids doesn't mean they don't have power. Even young people can write letters that get people to act. Years ago, for instance, kids helped change things for the better for dolphins. Before the days of dolphin-safe tuna nets, huge numbers of dolphins were killed when tuna were caught. Kids wrote letters, boycotted school lunches and made people listen. I tell my students, 'If you learn about something and care about it, share your ideas. It can do great things.' I try to show students that learning often means putting your knowledge to work to help others. When you have knowledge, you have the power to make things better for people, animals and the environment." That is what teaching is all about for this talented educator.

Could You Have a Career as a Classroom Teacher?

Do you enjoy learning and sharing your knowledge with others? Do you enjoy sharing your knowledge about animals in particular? If so, a career as a classroom teacher with a humane focus might be the job for you. Here are some ideas for further exploration:

1. What is it really like to be a teacher? Interview one or more of your teachers to find out. Learn all you can about teaching and share this information in a class project or report.

2. You can practice being a teacher right now. Get on-the-job experience by tutoring a younger or less experienced student. Ask your teacher, reading specialist or school librarian about how to get started.

3. Find out more about teaching by writing to the National Education Association, 1201 16th St., NW, Washington, D.C. 20036. Ask for the brochure "Make It Happen." You can also visit their website at http://www.nea.org/.

chapter 31
HSUS'S EXECUTIVE OFFICER

As the spokesperson for the largest animal protection organization in the country, HSUS Executive Vice President Patricia Forkan helps animals in numerous ways.

Enter the main building of The Humane Society of the United States (HSUS) in Washington, D.C., and you won't see any animals. What you will see is an office with computer terminals, fax machines and more than one hundred busy, dedicated employees. Founded in 1954, The HSUS is a nonprofit organization that helps a wide variety of animals in many ways.

"We help animals through education, legislation and investigation," says HSUS executive vice president Patricia Forkan. "We publish books and brochures to teach people about animal needs. We put on workshops and classes for the public. We help people pass laws to protect animals. And, our investigators work to stop cruelty around the country and around the world." At the center of all these efforts is the executive vice president.

"There are two main ways in which my work helps animals," says Patricia. "I oversee people in the organization and work with people outside the organization." Her leadership role is important. "I oversee people's projects. I give them guidance. I help develop campaigns," she explains.

For instance, The HSUS started a campaign to encourage people to use cruelty-free cosmetics. This is makeup that has not been tested on animals. The HSUS cruelty-free cosmetics campaign educated people about this issue. It raised their interest in doing something about animal testing. Today a number of cosmetic companies have agreed to stop testing products on animals. Patricia played a major role in developing the cruelty-free cosmetics campaign.

"Each day brings a new problem or idea that must be acted upon," says Patricia. "I spend most of my time in meetings without ever looking at an animal up close. In overseeing so many projects, I must ask, 'How does each one meet our goals and what will it cost?'"

Another way Patricia helps animals is by working with people outside The HSUS. She works with government officials in this country and abroad. She goes to many international meetings where decisions about animals are made. The International Whaling Commission (IWC), for instance, has a meeting every year. Officials from countries all around the world attend. Some countries want to hunt whales. Others do not want whales to be hunted at all. The group decides which whales may be hunted and which will be protected. Patricia goes to these meetings to represent the interests of the whales.

Patricia's work demands that she be a good listener, that she have a good memory for details and that she be a problem-solver. "There is always more than one way to approach a challenge," she explains. "Understanding this is part of being a problem-solver." In Patricia's job, some of the problems she encounters are between people who have very different ideas about how animals should be treated. To work out the differences between these people, she needs to listen carefully. "When people disagree, you start by helping them see what they can agree on," says Patricia. "From that, you may be able to work out an understanding that will be good for animals."

Patricia also gives speeches at many of the meetings she attends. "A person in my position needs to be comfortable speaking in front of large numbers of people," she explains. "My words need to persuade or encourage others to help animals." Additionally, anyone who is interested in a leadership role in a national humane organization will need to have at least an undergraduate degree. Courses in political science, history and management are all helpful. Experience in legislation can be valuable as well.

When Patricia helps to develop an international agreement that protects thousands of animals—such as whales—she feels a real sense of accomplishment. She is pleased that her job helps humans as well as animals in many ways. "The HSUS also has many programs that affect people," she says. "We provide disaster relief, help students who believe it is wrong to dissect animals, teach people to be responsible pet owners, develop better laws, and help the environment by protecting habitat as well as saving endangered species—to name a few." Her favorite thing about her work is that "every day brings a new challenge. There are no dull moments," she says.

Like many people whose careers help animals, Patricia has had some unique experiences. At one point, she was traveling in Africa as part of her work. She had the opportunity to observe animals in the wild. "It was very moving to see African animals in their natural habitat," she says. "I had no idea that the animals you see in a zoo are just shadows of the creatures living in the wild."

Patricia has met many famous people who care about animals. She watched whales off the coast of South America with scientist Dr. Roger Payne. "We spotted a right whale in the distance," says Patricia. "He was headed in our direction. It was the first time I had been so close to a whale. I was fascinated. Yet it was also scary. The whale was the size of a city bus. And he was headed straight for the boat! Before we knew it, he made a sudden dive and went underneath us. I have never been so terrified and yet so full of joy and wonder at the same time. To see an animal as large as a whale watch you, as you are watching him, is a thrilling experience."

Leadership skills, like any skills, take practice. It is not always easy to work with others. It is not always easy to be a good listener and a problem-solver. Yet these are the primary skills of the executive officer of any national humane organization. If you care as much about helping animals as Patricia Forkan does, this demanding job can also be very rewarding. Who knows? You might one day put your own leadership skills to work for a national animal protection organization like The Humane Society of the United States.

Could You Have a Career as a
Humane Organization Executive Officer?

Could a job like Patricia Forkan's be right for you? One way to decide is to put your leadership skills to the test. You can start by exploring some of these ideas:

1. Talk to your teacher about what your class can do to help animals and the environment. Then, organize and lead a class effort to raise money for a local animal shelter, clean up a nearby wildlife habitat, plant a butterfly garden at your school or inform the public about an important local animal issue.

2. Give your leadership skills additional opportunity to grow. If there is no animal protection club at your school, try starting one. For ideas on how to get started, write to the National Association for Humane and Environmental Education (NAHEE), Box 362, East Haddam, CT 06423. Ask for a copy of the *Student Action Guide*.

3. Find out more about the work of The Humane Society of the United States, the largest animal protection organization in the country, by writing to them at 2100 L Street, NW, Washington, D.C. 20037, or by visiting their website at http://www.hsus.org/.

Index

"Afternoon of a Fawn" 131
AIDS 40
Alaska 109
All Creatures Great and Small 67
All Things Bright and Beautiful 67
All Things Wise and Wonderful 67
American Sign Language 102-104
American Society for the Prevention of Cruelty to Animals 39, 40
American Veterinary Medical Association 67
amphibians 97
anesthesia 55, 64, 70
animal behavior 65, 74, 79-80, 85
animal communication 37, 85, 92-93, 101-105
animal communication specialist 92-93, 101-105
animal control agency director 17-20
Animal Doctors 43
Animal Legal Defense Fund 165
Animal Protection Society of Orange County 80
animal shelter 40, 73
animal shelter veterinarian 39-43
antifreeze 68
Arand, Dr. Thomas 54-57
artist 131, 148-152
ASPCA 39-43
Association of Pet Dog Trainers 82
Austin, Texas 96, 97
Backyard Birds 152
banding 92
Bat conservation International 96-100
Batman: Exploring the World of Bats 100
bats 96-99
beaver dams, living near 123
Beaver Defenders 123
beavers 121-124, 145
Beckstead, Scott 162-165
Benjamin, Carol Lea 82
Bergh, Henry 40
Bevan, Laura 44-47
bird feeders 113
Bird Watcher's Digest 149
Bird Watching for Dummies 152
birds 97, 112, 117, 118
Brant, Lori Paradis 116-119
breed rescue groups 88
Burns, Pamela 12-15

butterfly garden 171, 183
Buyukmichi, Hope Sawyer 121-126
California 134
career awareness 2
Carolina parakeet 151
Chapel Hill, North Carolina 79
Chimpanzee and Human Communication Institute 103
chimpanzees 101
chipmunks 124
Church, Ann 166-169
Cole, Earlene 35-38
Columbus, Ohio 88
Connecticut Audubon Society 116-120
Cook, Christine 170-174
Cornell College of Veterinary Medicine 41
Cricket 149
cruelty-free cosmetics 181
Curtis, Patricia 43
Dar 102-104
Debussy, Claude 131
deer 60, 124, 171
Destreza, Kathryn 21-24
disaster relief specialist 9, 44-48
dissection, refusing to do 104
dog bites, preventing 56
Dog Training for Kids 82
dolphins 107, 110
Drawing on the Right Side of the Brain 152
earthworms 118
ecosystem 97
EcoWomen: Protectors of the Earth 105
Edwards, Betty 152
elephants 104
environment, protecting the 98, 99, 118
environmental educator 93, 116-120
Environmental Media Corporation 139-143
ethology, definition 104
euthanasia 14, 163
Explorers' Post 11
Exxon Valdez oil spill 109
falcon, peregrine 112
farm animals 35-38
Forkan, Patricia 180-183
Fort Wayne Department of Animal Care and Control 17-20

Fort Wayne, Indiana 17
Fouts, Dr. Roger and Deborah 101-104
freelance employment 132
Freisen, Eugene 154
Friends of Washoe 101-105
Garcia, David 25-29
Goodall, Dr. Jane 100
gorillas 104
habitats 142, 146
Halley, Paul 154
Harrar, George and Linda 105
Harvard University 150
Hawaii 13
Hawaiian Humane Society, The 12-15
Hawk Mountain 113
hawks 112, 113, 114
herons 124
Herriot, James 67
Honolulu 13
Houston SPCA 25-29
Houston, Texas 26
HSUS executive officer 180-183
HSUS-WRTC 58-62
human-animal bond 56
humane education, definition 31
humane educator 7-8, 30-34
humane investigator 25-29
humane landscape designer 158, 161, 170-174
humane officer 6-7, 21-24
humane society director 12-16
Humane Society of Missouri 35-38
Humane Society of the United States, The 45, 48, 51, 60, 115
iguanas 119
Independent Pet and Animal Transportation Association 90
insects 98, 118
Jane's Vet Clinic 68
jellyfish 140
kestrels 113
KIND News 32, 34
Klein, Dr. Patrice 58-62
Ladybug 149
Large Animal Rehabilitation Center (LARC) 35
large animal shelter director 35-38
large animal veterinarian 63-67
law enforcement 6, 19, 26
laws 167, 168
lawyer 158, 162-165
leadership 15

Lewis, Belinda 17-20
lobbyist 158, 166-169
Long, Barbara 78-81
Louisiana SPCA 21-24
Loulis 102-104
Marine Mammal Center 106-110
marine mammal stranding specialist 93, 106-110
Marshall County Animal Rescue League 31-34
Michelsen, Dr. Paul 63-66
Miller, Dr. Lila 39-43
Millington, New Jersey 111
minnows 122
Moja 102-104
Mossaics 170-174
musician 131, 153-156
NAHEE 183
National Association for Humane and Environmental Education 32
National Association of Dog Obedience Instructors 75, 82
National Association of Pet Sitters 86
Native American tradition 27
naturalist 93, 116-120
nature 114, 117
nature centers 117
Nature Conservancy 150
New Orleans, 21
New York City 39, 88
Newfield, New Jersey 122
Nimoy, Leonard 155
North American Nature Photography Association 138
North American Veterinary Technician Association 72
nuthatches 124
obedience trainer 74-75, 78-82
oil spills 137
owls 112, 113, 124
Paw in Hand 78-82
Payne, Dr. Roger 154, 182
Payne, Katharine 105
Pease, Donna 83-86
Pendergraft, Bill 139-143
Pennsylvania 113
pet bereavement 14
pet needs 23
Pet Sitters International 86
Pet Taxi 87-90
pet taxi driver 76, 87-90
pet-sitter 75-76, 83-86

Philadelphia 88
photographer 128, 134-138
police 22
Potter Valley, California 63
predators 98
Pringle, Lawrence
Raptor Trust, The 111-115
Reilly, Larry 87-90
Rogers, Will 49
Round Rock, Texas 54
Ryden, Hope, books by
   ABC of Crawlers and Flyers
   America's Bald Eagles
   Backyard Rescue
   The Beaver
   Bobcat
   Joey: The Story of a Baby Kangaroo
   Little Deer of the Florida Keys
   Out of the Wild: The story of Domesticated Animals
   Wild Horse Summer
   Your Cat's Wild Cousins
   Your Dog's Wild Cousins
Ryden, Hope 144-147
safety 37, 98
Sampson, Ron 68-71
Sausalito, California 107
Scanlon, Barbara 30-34
scat 120
sea lions 107, 108
sea otters 107, 109
sea turtles 141
seals 106, 107
Shakespeare 153
shelters 5-10
sign language 102-104
Signs of the Apes, Songs of the Whales: Adventures in Human-Animal Communication 105
Sirch, Willow Ann 105
Smith, Dawn 106-109
Smithsonian Institution 98
snakes 97, 114
Soucy, Diane 113
Soucy, Dr. Len 111-114
Spaying and neutering, importance of 14, 18, 23
Spider 149
squirrels 124
Student Action Guide 183

suggested activities 16, 20, 24, 29, 34, 38, 43, 48, 57, 62, 67, 72, 100, 105, 110, 115, 120, 125, 138, 143, 147, 152, 156, 165, 169, 174, 179, 183
surgery 55, 56
swallows 124
Talbot, Bob 134-138
teacher 160-161, 175-179
Tendercare Pet-Sitting 83-86
The Humane Society of the United States 44-48, 166-169, 180-183
The Lord God Made Them All 67
Tracy, Carol 175-179
turtle 58-59, 118
Tuttle, Dr. Merlin 96-100
U.S. Fish and Wildlife Service 59
Unexpected Wildlife Refuge 121-125
Valez, Glen 154
Velcro 102
veterinarian 8, 39-43, 49-67, 107
veterinary assistant 52
veterinary technician 40, 51-52, 68-72, 106-109
video producer 129, 139-142
Washington, D.C. 68
Washoe 102-104
websites 34, 67, 72, 82, 100, 105, 110, 138, 143, 147, 152, 156, 165, 169, 174, 178, 183
West Virginia University 32
whales 104, 107, 110, 134
whales 134
Wild Neighbors: The Humane Approach to Living with Wildlife 115
wildlife biologist 92, 96-100, 154
wildlife gardening 172, 174
wildlife refuge manager 93, 121-125
wildlife rehabilitator 93, 107, 111-115
wildlife veterinarian 58-62
Winter, Paul 153-156
Winter, Paul, recordings by
   Callings
   Canyon
   Earth: Voices of a Planet
   Prayer for the Wild Things
   Whales Alive!
   Wolf Eyes: A Retrospective
women and veterinary training 41
wood ducks 124
writer 130, 144-147
Zickefoose, Julie 148-152
zoo 182